SELF-EXAMINATION

SELF-EXAMINATION

On the Journey to the End

T. HOOGSTEEN

RESOURCE *Publications* · Eugene, Oregon

SELF-EXAMINATION
On the Journey to the End

Copyright © 2022 T. Hoogsteen. All rights reserved. Except for brief quotations in critical publications or reviews, no part of this book may be reproduced in any manner without prior written permission from the publisher. Write: Permissions, Wipf and Stock Publishers, 199 W. 8th Ave., Suite 3, Eugene, OR 97401.

Resource Publications
An Imprint of Wipf and Stock Publishers
199 W. 8th Ave., Suite 3
Eugene, OR 97401

www.wipfandstock.com

PAPERBACK ISBN: 978-1-6667-3619-9
HARDCOVER ISBN: 978-1-6667-9420-5
EBOOK ISBN: 978-1-6667-9421-2

JANUARY 7, 2022 11:37 AM

Scripture quotations are from the Holy Bible, English Standard Version, © 2001 by Crossway Bibles, a publishing ministry of Good News Publishers. All rights reserved.

Taran William
Kaitlin Christine

Aiyanna Joy

Katriel Lynn

Haleigh Ann

Jaden Daniel

Charlotte Taylor

Zoë Morgan

For insight

Contents

Preface | ix

INTRODUCTION | 1

IN THE WEST INITIALLY | 14

IN THE WEST HORIZONTALLY | 20

IN THE WEST VERTICALLY | 30

FINALLY | 135

Bibliography | 139

Preface

This is the West.
This is you.
You draw the whole of the West into yourselves.
You are the Western dreams, the loves, the greeds, and the hurts.
You are its indulgences, contradictions, perversions, and stupidities all in one.

This fMRI-like file of pictures may please you, even polish your self-esteem.
The whole system of impressions may displease you.
Each character analysis gives a mini-impression of yourselves gazing, staring intensely back at you.

This *SELF-EXAMINATION* is about dispassionate self-examination,
peering sharply and persistently into your Western soul,
daringly exposing its innermost workings.

Here, too, all errors and damages of imperialism and racism,
including the injuries to minorities,
you will own.
Westerners share in the responsibilities of pursuing mammonism.

You please the powers of the age.
You make yourselves look good.
You justify yourselves in the presence of the Western gods and goddesses.
By living the standards of the West you are good for a purpose:
you live and work to make your self-esteem glow,
only to please current deities.

Introduction

These are not the brightest days. In positive times the future looks bright, even though none know tomorrow. In negative times the future looks dark. Westerners, as they double-down on the migratory order, cling to the only known way of life. Generationally, people of the West move irresistibly into the dark electro-magnetic heart of this civilization.

> The migratory order is a command harder than steel and a temptation softer than down, neither of which brooks resistance.

This irresistible attraction constitutes the world's power, 1 John 2:16. None in the West falter in this ceaseless migration into the Western heart and its unrelenting religiosities. The West as any other civilization forms an alternative to the Kingdom, each civilization born out of unbelief to house idolatries.

At the crossroads of life the Church as a Western institution and all believers as Western citizens intentionally and actively submit to the migratory order. Newcome immigrants begin this journeying the moment they set foot in the West, duplicating what generations of deeply rooted citizens do. However, easing along into Westernization by obeying the migratory order opposes the rigors of maturing in the Faith.

To break with the descent into the Western heart of absolute darkness, darkness without ever a dawn, the Lord Jesus summons believers to self-examination. This always painful process never reverses the journeying. It is to pilgrimage away from and out of Western cultures into the Kingdom of Heaven, alias, the Kingdom of God, Christ Jesus' rule. Through self-examination believers (come to) know the full extent of the in-the-world/not-of-the-world tensions and pressures—without jumping off the globe, John 17:11, 15; 1 Corinthians 5:10.

Christ's Kingdom is wherever believers together and individually out of thankfulness for salvation obey his rule, explicitly. First John 3:3.

Self-Examination

V

On the First Day of the creation week the Christ in conjunction with God the Father and God the Holy Spirit—Trinity in unity—revealed his universal rule, which on earth he called his Kingdom. Before the Incarnation[1] he summoned Adam, Noah,[2] Abraham, Moses, and David to govern the Kingdom in his name. Falling prey to idolatries, David's descendants over centuries ruined the Kingdom to the point of extinction. Then throughout his ministry, while restricting and restraining the glory of his divinity, Philippians 2:1–8, the Christ restored his rule, in the process calling all of sinful Israel to follow him, through them to manifest the Kingdom. During the ordeal of the Incarnation-Crucifixion-Resurrection event he 1) recreated his humanity gloriously, and 2) earned righteousness for his people. Righteousness, first of all, constitutes the removal of guilt for every sin, large and small, his people committed. Then, upon the Ascension, he resumed his exalted rulership earlier revealed in the Old Testament dispensation, Isaiah 6:1–5, now as God and man, divine and human. In the hour of the Ascension he took from the hand of God the Father the scroll in and on which inscribed the continuing course of history, with the Kingdom the active wedge, Revelation 5:6–8. By way of that scroll God the Father recognized Jesus in his humanity and divinity as God the Son; that is, from the beginning the Lord of heaven and earth constituted from out of the Church his rule of righteousness, peace, and joy in the Holy Spirit. As in the Old Testament dispensation so in the New Testament, the manifestation of the Kingdom creates the flesh and blood of the Church's preaching.

Through the preaching the Christ from the glorious place of rulership at the right hand of God the Father reveals the mighty works of his dominion, the course of history, the liveliness of the center of the Kingdom, the Church, and the imputation of his righteousness, thereby equipping his people for service in the Kingdom, Ephesians 3:14–19, 4:11–13. Righteousness, crucial to every aspect of Kingdom work, the Scriptures reveal as Romans 3:21–25a; Ephesians 2:4–7; etc. Accentuating the Romans passage,

> But now the righteousness of God has been manifested apart from the law, although the Law and the Prophets bear witness to it—the

---

1. Through the Incarnation the Christ assumed human nature, enfleshment, which made him in his Person both God and man.

2. The global deluge from which the Christ rescued Noah's Eight served as a precursor to the first and great Judgment, 1 Peter 3:18; 2 Peter 3:5–7.

INTRODUCTION

righteousness of God through faith in Jesus Christ for all who believe. For there is no distinction: for all have sinned and fall short of the glory of God, and are justified by his grace as a gift, through the redemption that is in Christ Jesus, whom God put forward as a propitiation by his blood, to be received by faith.

This the Son of God earned throughout the three years of his ministry, crucially during the Crucifixion, when in his humanity he absorbed the punishment for the sins of his people and cleansed away the guilt of sinning. Now from the vantage point of his holy dominion he imputes his righteousness in the Church through the preaching.

\/

How you now self-evaluate and assess your inner landscapes depends in a major way on your journeying according to the migratory order. The more you assimilate Western culture and immerse yourselves in this way of life—in whatever Western country and with whatever Western neighbors—the more you recognize that you are one with all of the West. The adaptation of the Western way of life builds secular self-esteem: you feel good about yourselves. In other words, your thoughts and your commitments and your activities earn you self-righteousness, or works-righteousness. You make yourselves righteous.

In flagrant contrast to the righteousness in Christ, unbelievers seek self-righteousness, which consists of good works; these good works make unbelievers think well of themselves plus they expect that the Western gods and goddesses wholeheartedly agree. Through good works unbelievers plan to make enough of an impression upon gods and goddesses worshiped that these accept them in respective communions. As individuals and as communities of unbelievers the self-righteous consider themselves a grade or two above others. Such were the sneering Pharisees/Sadducees who resisted the Christ to the utmost, lest he impute his merited righteousness upon the Israelites they dominated.

Additional to Westerners who find satisfaction in secular self-esteem, there are in the Church those who claim on the one hand salvation by grace (alone); yet on the other find they have to add a little effort to the righteousness in Christ to make sure he won't bypass them.

Such works-righteousness makes you feel good about yourselves; in addition you merit space in the neighborhoods of the current religious powers. Hence, as you day-by-day build up your Curriculum Vitae (CV)

Self-Examination

or resumé, you hope that your works-righteousness may be acceptable to the larger-than-life deities you worship. However, here's the thing. How you, individually and communally, weigh your self-righteousness matters little. In the West's journeying to the end the Christ judges you in his all-determinative manner. Since the first and great Judgment, he clarified his judgments—at each death and in the end—first on the Westernizing Church. This judging concentrates indomitably in the preaching, with vision of depth.

The Judge of heaven and earth through the extreme pains of self-examination exposes church members' hearts—each one and all—who they are in him. In shedding the ways of the West and by resolutely pilgrimaging into the Kingdom, the light of the first and great Judgment, the Crucifixion, reveals the essential believers. His judging is holy, contrary to the covetousness of Western civilization. In the process of self-examination, then, the glories of Jesus' Second Advent break through.

\/

For self-examination many parts of the Scriptures suffice, but for now consider and apply several mandatory initiatives from the *Gospel according to Matthew*, each of which with peremptory insistence penetrates into most stubborn hearts.

- Matthew 7:12, "So whatever you wish that others would do to you, do also to them, for this is the Law and the Prophets."
- Matthew 7:13–14, "Enter by the narrow gate (into the Kingdom of Heaven). For the gate is wide and the way is easy that leads to destruction, and those who enter by it are many. For the gate is narrow and the way is hard that leads to life, and those who find it are few."
- Matthew 7:24–27, "Everyone then who hears these words of [Jesus] and does them will be like a wise man who built his house on the rock. And the rain fell, and the floods came, and the winds blew and beat on that house, but it did not fall, because it had been founded on the rock. And everyone who hears these words of mine and does not do them will be like a foolish man who built his house on the sand. And the rains fell, and the floods came, and the winds blew and beat against that house, and it fell, and great was the fall of it."

INTRODUCTION

- Matthew 12:33–37, "Either make the tree good and its fruit good, or make the tree bad and its fruit bad. You brood of vipers! How can you speak good, when you are evil? For out of the abundance of the heart the mouth speaks. The good person out of his good treasure brings forth good, and the evil person out his evil treasure brings forth evil. I tell you, on the day of judgment people will give account for every careless word they speak. For by your words you will be justified, and by your words you will be condemned."

These Matthean texts constitute wisdom sayings, each of which pierces hearts, if not today then too late on the Day of Judgment. And the answers comprise the Christ's judgment upon also each and every Westerner, first and foremost the members of the Church, 1 Peter 4:17.

\/

With that judgment in mind and for self-examination, the current tilt of the West slants into socialism>communism,[3] away from Modernist rationalism, capitalist rigors, post-1945 revolutionary upheavals, and other furious agitations of disorder; new generations aspire for security by submission to anti-Western, socialist forces. In the face of present uncertainties and violent dissensions the promises of socialism>communism have appeal. The political gradient into peace at (almost) any price now slides into the satisfactions and pleasures of letting governments make the difficult decisions with fatherly or motherly sorts of care. These contemporary social judgements, to allow governments and idolatrous commitments to make the main decisions, align the descent along the migratory order.

Not only to halt the descent down the migratory order, but directly step without vacillation into the Christ's Kingdom describes the utility of *SELF-EXAMINATION*. For this purpose *SELF-EXAMINATION* in its *VERTICALLY* chapter constitutes a file of fMRI[4] films of all going down the migratory way, unware of and unfamiliar with, even unwilling to visualize

---

3. Shapiro, *The Authoritarian Moment*, 4, "Something there is in man that loves a dictator."

Shapiro, *On the Right Side of History*, 16, "Tyranny rarely begins with jackboots; it usually begins with ardent wishes for a better future, combined with an unfailing faith in the power of mass mobilization." 21, "[It's] leaders suggest that we live in a world of destructive chaos—that there is no plan, no progress, no personal accountability. They've argued that we are nothing more than victims of the systems into which we are born—we are inescapably earthbound."

4. Functional Magnetic Resonance Imaging.

Self-Examination

the untamed darkness of death at the end of the road. As you see yourselves in these films as Westerners caught up in, enthralled by, enmeshed in, or relishing the promises of the socialist>communist trajectory, or see yourselves moving into a pleasantly changing socialist comfort zone, you also find yourselves evolving, little by little, for instance, accepting socialist sexual behaviors, socialist Sunday standards, socialist vocabularies, or socialist politics. In these times, as you see yourselves descending along the migratory way, remember, in Christ Jesus there is no east or west. There is also no political right or political left, only the ascent of the Kingdom. Through self-examination he summons his own to leave the cultures of the West that domineeringly cling to Christians going down by the migratory order into the heart of darkness, now transiting into socialism>communism. The only way out begins by pilgrimaging into the light of the Kingdom.

To make self-examination difficult, Westerners from one end of this physical mass to the other, involuntarily and then voluntarily listen on the way down to a musical whispering that transcends right-wing and left-wing politics; the sounds come from inner-self sources. "We are a good people." Pleasing reverberations by the thousands of this humming constantly lay bare the covetousness at the core of this self-evaluation.[5] Such singing sounds align by default every Westerner with that soothing undertone, thus shaping everyone's cultural mindfulness—"We are, each one and all, morally upright people, rationally sound, and acceptable to the Western deities." Everyone in the West subscribes to these guiding thoughts by echolalia, repetitiously listening to or singing along with the Western soul's heartbeat drumming. In odd moments, admission of a problem or even a shame may slip out. But serious faults and humiliating shortcomings? Westerners find themselves single-mindedly and instinctively striving for stronger evidence of self-righteous, exactly the vulnerability the Western deities endorse and therefore bless. Westerners experience in this facile esteem authorized by the gods and goddesses the pleasantly rippling effects of submitting to the migratory order.

By self-examination believers discard Western norms, values, institutional memberships, and language patterns typical of this civilization. They strip off and throw away the remaining traces of Modernism's anti-Christianity, then fight against socialism's lures. Believers spurn the ways of self-esteem>self-righteousness that despise the Gospel. In the sanctifying

---

5. Harari, *Homo Deus*, 262, "Most psychologists believe that only human feelings are authorised to determine the true meaning of human actions."

process, all in Christ, reading, *ingest* the Scriptures as the food and drink of the life, the truth, and the way of the Kingdom.

\/

Two judgments in the Scriptures lay out human destiny. Old Testament history led up to the first and great, the Crucifixion; on the Cross the Christ earned the salvation of the elect. At the same time he announced the condemnation of the reprobate, the controversial people whom he from the Genesis beginning bypassed and left to earn their own righteousness. Thus, upon Adam's Fall the first and great Judgment revealed forever the only two constituent peoples, they who believe the Christ's Atonement and they who reject the Gospel. The second and last Judgment reveals the actuality of the first and determinative verdict; at that glorious hour the consequences of the Crucifixion, first the eternal dividing-line, make plain the distinction between the elect and the reprobate, the latter too busy proving the defeat in sinning.

The Christ now directs the West to the final edge of history, then, beginning within the Church, to expose Westerners for who they are. Hence,

> . . . the heavens and earth that now exist are stored up for fire, being kept until the day of judgment and destruction of the ungodly.
> 2 Peter 3:7

The West living and moving and breathing between the two judgments day-by-day approaches the second and last, while carrying away the Church in its bosom.

\/

Upon the Resurrection and after the Ascension, Jesus (through Apostle Paul, for one) announced the elemental promise of the Gospel in its New Testament format, elsewhere also, but for the present purpose, more focused, Romans 3:21–22,

> But now the righteousness of God has been manifested apart from the [Oral Law], although the Law and the Prophets bear witness to it—the righteousness of God through faith in Jesus Christ for all who believe.
> Habakkuk 2:4

Self-Examination

This righteousness Jesus imputes, unilaterally imposes. Thereby he transforms unbelievers into believers: *you are now free from the guilt of sinning, the punishment for which I suffered in the agony of the Crucifixion*. This imputation of righteousness is a divine work, totally, enacted apart from the exercise of the human will, except to change that will. All have sinned, which involves misaligning the will too. Christian righteousness comes only through imposition, spurning every conception of the freedom of the will.

V

To reveal the perfect rectitude of the original separation between the elect and the reprobate, Christ Jesus on the basis of the Crucifixion revealed and reveals throughout the Church another partitioning, now among his people. In this process of separation he displays to the world of reprobates the impacting fairness of divine judging.

1–3. In the Church some members believe the Gospel and live the consequent life by stepping out of the migratory order, however broken the attempts. By way of or because of that brokenness they followed the migratory order into the Western heart, into the darkness of unbelief. The ease and comfortableness of the migratory order at relaxing incrementally the doctrines and ethics of Christianity please heart, soul, mind, and body; the appeal of worldliness gratifies even strongest believers.[6] To be in the world and not off the world raises most sensitive and difficult existential moments. Deny the Christ? Impugn salvation? Break his Commandments? Examining life by way of sanctification is hard, exhaustive and tiresome.

The Christ calls believers on the way down into the Western heart to self-examination; he shows each one the fMRI films he takes of their unbelieving descent into worldliness. In that surrendering to worldliness, the Lord and Savior calls his own to repentance and real amendment, to recognize the pain of sinning and acknowledge the grace of imputed righteousness, " . . . so that he may establish your hearts blameless in holiness before our God and Father," 1 Thessalonians 3:13. Thus the Christ by the proclamation of the Word and through the Holy Spirit pulls sinners back from and out of the overwhelming adversities of the migratory order into the rectitude of the Faith, for now the never-ending toil of pilgrimaging

---

6. Fukuyama, *Identity*, 54, "With the decline during the twentieth century in Western societies of a shared belief in Christianity, different rules and values from other cultures began displacing traditional ones, as well as the option of not believing at all."

INTRODUCTION

called sanctification, another substantive of Sunday preaching. Believers thus stand back and recognize the persuasiveness of as well as the provocative sting of sinning. Departing from the command mentality of the West into the Kingdom on the journey to the end defines Christianity. For this self-examination the dominant question stands out:

> Who are you/we before Christ Jesus?

If you conflate what you think of your Western selves with what the Christ thinks of you and then blithely continue down the migratory order you only fool yourselves.

2–3. Opposite those whom the Christ declares righteous are the self-righteous, members of the Church who hear but do not hear the Gospel, nevertheless imagining that they believe; these people build a righteousness based on a temporary faith, Mark 4:5–6, or a historical faith, Mark 4:7, by which they live to please gods other than the Christ or his Father, never knowing the sanctificatory work of the Holy Spirit. Arrogantly, they presume believing the Gospel while adding up formidably important *good* works, which they hope will please the deities they actually worship.

Jesus, divine and human, matured within Israel's framework of religiosity, the whole of which infused by and overcome with Pharisaism; its leaders from out of synagogues led the people of the covenant in the service of the Beelzebul or Satan, Matthew 12:26–27, John 8:39–46, 44 specifically. By living according to the prescriptions of the Oral Law and hating the Christ they build up self-esteem into poisonous self-righteousness; by works of obedience structured according to the Oral Law they presumed to be righteous in the eyes of the god worshiped. Jesus knew the self-righteousness of this people well.

The self-righteous, currently holding membership in the Church, do a few of the Commandments superficially, hereby planning to please the ones they serve. Outwardly those collected and diligently archived proofs of self-righteousness look good; these members are never caught breaking one of the few laws they hold dear. Externally they conform to the living of respective congregations. Slowly, however, by the imperative code of the West they willfully and comfortably slide down the migratory order towards the Western heart. Self-righteousness wills a comfortable religiosity.

In the hour of death, or if they live long enough, at the second and last Judgment, Jesus shows these church members the fMRI films of their worldliness, proof sufficient of reprobation and for condemnation. They, "to fill up the measure of their sins," 1 Thessalonians 2:16, follow the migratory order into the disreputable heart of Western unbelief without even momentary remorse. Subsequently they have no claim on the righteousness the Christ agonizingly earned, thus demonstrating in and to the world of reprobates that he judges and condemns righteously, never erring.

3–3. Again, also opposite the righteousness the Christ created on the Cross, in the Church are unbelievers who carelessly pursue the migratory order. To avoid the irritations of the Gospel they find one excuse or another to walk out of the Church and make the migratory order stress-free, Mark 4:4, and join the reprobate billions across the West. Second Thessalonians 2:11–12, "Therefore God sends them a strong delusion, so that they may believe what is false, in order that all may be condemned who did not believe the truth but had pleasure in unrighteousness." When these dissidents die or finally stand before the Judge in the second and last Judgment, Jesus shows from the various books, Revelation 20:12, all fMRI slides of their living, proof beyond doubt of reprobation and for condemnation, plea bargaining unthinkable.

The self-righteous at departing from the covenant community pluck from thousands of possibilities individualized standards by which to measure self-worth and promote self-importance in the eyes of respective gods, which essentially are no gods at all, only aristocratic powers of the age. In worlds of reprobates this condemnation of the self-righteous will be considered fair.

Summarily, by works accomplished during the migratory order degenerating Westerners persuade the powers that be of the acceptable goodness they earn. Specifically, achieving this feel-good self-righteousness makes them acceptable in the eyes of domesticated gods and goddesses. Now, living and moving between the two fundamental judgments, from the first and great Judgment to the second and last, all Westerners find themselves in the closing approach to the moment of standing before the Christ, believers only committed to the painful stresses of self-examination and real amendment.

ASSIMILATIVE THOUGHTS

With respect to the future of the West, thinkers with thick volumes predicted the imminent end, a total collapse, in the horrors of the moment real amendment impossible, the entire civilization tipping over a steep

INTRODUCTION

precipice into oblivion on a noxious landfill site. In such assumptions Western civilization follows the long-deceased Roman Empire of faraway history, which forecasting seems reprehensible.[7] Limiting the immediate horizon of the West with an expiry date crosses an ethical line fraught with hubris. See: Oswald Spengler's 1918 *The Decline of the West*. See: Arnold J. Toynbee's 1934–1961 *A Study of History* and 1948 *Civilization on Trial*.[8] In contrast the *On the Journey to the End* qualifier never suggests that the West is ready to fall over a cliff and pollute the earth with another combustible pile of thrash.[9] Predictions as Spengler and Toynbee's only stir up painful anxieties,[10] depressive torpors, and fickle rebellions that immunize against self-examination. A providentially ongoing West, however, makes real amendment more necessary.

Any factual exposition of the West's intellectual, moral, and cultural climate supposes, as does self-examination, trust in its longevity, however much this assertion fights insecurities of doubt. Appositive to the West's

---

7. Hedges, *America*, 6, "That the end is coming is hard now to dispute, although one would be foolish to predict when."

Mishra, *Bland Fanatics*, 13, "The world as we have known it, moulded by the beneficiaries of both Western imperialism and anti-imperialist nationalism, is crumbling."

Winchester, *Pacific*, 424, "These days the planet is witnessing a sudden and wholesale redistribution of world power, one that is unprecedented in its speed. It is experiencing a shift in emphasis that suggests that this Western dominance, especially in the regions where such was both unquestioned and unquestionable, may now, and quite rapidly, be coming to an end."

8. Toynbee, *Civilization On Trial*, 13, "After two hundred and fifty years of comparative tranquility, the Empire suffered in the third century of the Christian era a collapse from which it never fully recovered, and at the next crisis, in the fifth and sixth centuries, it went to pieces irretrievably."

Ferguson, *Doom*, 204, "Empires are the most complex of all political units that humans have constructed, precisely because they seek to exert power over very large areas and diverse cultures."

9. Remember Nikita Khrushchev's, "We will bury you!"?

10. Huntington, *The Clash of Civilizations*, 20, "The balance of power among the civilizations is shifting: the West is declining in relative influence; Asian civilizations are expanding their economic, military, and political strength; Islam is exploding demographically with destabilizing consequences for Muslim countries and their neighbors; and non-Western civilizations generally are reaffirming the values of their own cultures."

Hedges, *America*, 294, "The American empire is coming to an end. The nation has lost the power and respect needed to induce allies in Europe, Latin America, Asia, and Africa to do its bidding."

tragic death, *On the Journey to the End* supposes continuous changing—change upon change, change within change, and change through change.[11]

Recognizing in many places restlessness caused by the movement from atheistic Renaissance>Enlightenment>Modernism into the grasping arms of atheistic socialism>communism, the instability of the West gathers force sliding over the edge into a different Western civilization. As the one ages and weakens, the other strengthens in pulling Westernism in a different way into the archaic and fetid heart of this civilization.

\/

Upon the *Preface* and *Initially*, follows the first main part, *Horizontally*, a topographical overview of the West; this synopsis physically demonstrates the West's transitory nature. The whole of this civilization restlessly slides over naked edges of change; physical distortions, catastrophic or invisible, marking out destructive torments and remorseless social movements. The second main part, *Vertically*, opens up the West in a perpendicular way, taking a fMRI-like layered perspective; each (sub)titling exposes another *slice* of the Western soul for analyzing internal complications and complexities of your deadly peril descending along the migratory order. You may appreciate some slices of this fMRI file, denounce many. The conclusion, *Finally*, sets the West, the greatest civilization of all time, in the light of the Christ's Second Advent.

As you raise eyebrows at the fear factor of change in *SELF-EXAMINATION* pay attention to footnotes only when you reach an *Oh, really?!* moment; then stop and contemplate a quote or a clarification.

Also, if you sense a North American atmosphere in and about this monograph, specifically a Canadian, an explanation is easy. I live here; according to the flesh this is my large physical, mental, and emotional center of existence within Western civilization.

Herewith thanks to staff of the Brantford, Ontario, Public Library for opening hitherto unexplored areas of an amazing collection; through AD 2021 the library became a more fascinating institution.

---

11. Thunberg, *No One Is Too Small To Make a Difference*, 3–4, "To all of you who choose to look the other way every day because you seem more frightened of the changes that can prevent catastrophic climate change than the catastrophic climate change itself."

Jones, *Darwin's Ghost*, xviii, "The idea of life as fixed in a divine mold was dead. Instead, all was change."

Shapiro, *On the Right Side of History*, 13, "Darwinian evolution leaves no room for the true; it only leaves room for the evolutionary beneficial."

Introduction

Wife, Jayne, reading through the growing manuscript insisted that the whole remain biblically true, which constantly exercised my conscience.

In The West INITIALLY

WESTERN CIVILIZATION[1] IN CONTRAST to and in distinction from other such living entities trembles under weights of superlatives. Even hyperboles fail.[2] It is impressive. It is imposing. Economically, militarily, medically/surgically, culturally, educationally, technologically, democratically the West supersedes other civilizations—South American, African, Russian, Oriental, Middle Eastern/Islamic, Caribbean, Israeli,[3] subcontinent Indian, and even every Western indigenous construction of life.[4] From its Eurocentric roots to its American leadership,[5] the West presides over the earth. For the present yet its dominance sits seriously firm.[6]

---

1. Huntington, *The Clash of Civilizations*, 41, "Civilization and culture both refer to the overall way of life of a people, and a civilization is a culture writ large. They both involve the 'values, norms, institutions, and modes of thinking to which successive generations in a given society have attached primary importance.'" The quote comes from Fernand Braudel's *On History*, University of Chicago Press, 1980.

2. Tenold, *Everything You Love Will Burn*, 49, quoting Huntington, *The Clash of Civilizations*, "Every civilization sees itself as the center of the world and writes its history as the central drama of human history."

3. As much as Israel identifies with the West, America specifically, this nation and people historically stand apart, Rom 9:1–5.

4. Hedges, *America*, 259, "The foundation of that understanding of love and compassion for *Unci Maka*, that love for Mother Earth, understands the balance of the colors of the rainbow that encompass everyone. It's always been there. It's a search to find that patience and how we utilize our mind and heart. The longest journey sometimes is between the mind and the heart."

5. Morgan, *Australia*, 82, "... Australia gradually became more reliant on the USA as a superpower. The imperial connection with Britain continued but declined markedly after the Second World War."
Huntington, *The Clash of Civilizations*, 20–21, "The survival of the West depends on Americans reaffirming their Western identity and Westerners accepting their civilization as unique not universal and uniting to renew and preserve it against challenges from non-Western societies."

6. Ferguson, *Civilization*, 142, "From the middle of the nineteenth century until the

In The West Initially

Another feature defines the West's distinctiveness. Rather than a contiguous landmass, as Africa and the Middle East, Russia and China,[7] Western civilization's periphery circumscribes North America, Northern Europe, inclusive England and Ireland,[8] along with Australasia; its circumference wanders about against three other continents, making its physical presence felt internationally. Now, its boundaries no longer in motion, the sun never sets on Western civilization.[9]

The West holds its people together in cultural kinship by legal structures, adopted regulations, and unwritten responsibilities. Instructive identifiers of this civilization[10]—governments, courts, Germanic languages, dress codes, foods, religiosities, etc.—evolved over centuries by spellbinding accretions, which separated Westerners existentially

---

middle of the twentieth, the West ruled over the Rest. This was the age not just of empires but of imperialism, a theory of overseas expansion that justified the formal and informal domination of non-Western peoples on both self-interest and altruistic grounds."

7. Winchester, *Pacific*, 28, " . . . there is China—the world's most populous nation, fast ascending to the ladder tops, to the summits, of almost every measurable feature of modern humankind. This proud and ancient and imperturbable nation lies on the far side of the Pacific from America, the most powerful nation the world has ever known: it is easy to imagine that both are now glissading toward a rivalry and a possible confrontation that could easily end less than well for either party."

Harari, *Homo Deus*, 312, "China seems to offer a much more serious challenge than Western social protestors. Despite liberalising its politics and economics, China is neither a democracy nor a truly free-market economy, which does not prevent it from becoming the economic giant of the twenty-first century."

Manthorpe, *Claws of the Panda*, 3, "Whatever the Chinese Communist Party does, it does with Chinese characteristics. The management and style of the economy, the internal administration, the attitudes toward neighbouring and foreign states—these all owe more to Chinese traditions than to the country's experience of the outside world since the end of isolationism in the 1970s."

8. Toynbee, *Civilization On Trial*, 103, "In a certain sense, Europe still remains the centre of the world; and in a certain sense, again, the world is still being leavened by that Western civilization of which Western Europe is the original home."

9. Ferguson, *Civilization*, 142, "Empire meant 'living space' for surplus population. It meant secure export markets that a rival power could not enclose behind tariffs. It meant higher returns on investments than were available at home."

10. Thatcher, *The Downing Street Years*, 14, "It was the job of government to establish a framework of stability—whether constitutional stability, the rule of law, or the economic stability provided by sound money—within which individual families and businesses were free to pursue their own dreams and ambitions." 236, "Everyone talked about peace as if that in itself were the sole aim. But peace is not enough without freedom and justice and sometimes . . . it was necessary to sacrifice peace if freedom and justice were to prevail."

SELF-EXAMINATION

and visibly from other civilizations. The citizens of the West, affable one moment and crotchety the next, from country to country and region to region carry within and express without cultural affinities, economic as well as political and spiritual. Consider typical contrasts: they aspire to nobility and sink into cynicism, compete vigorously and guard privacy jealously, work hard and seek ease, as readily heal as kill, desire peace and equip for war, appreciate freedom and give in to slavery,[11] venerate science and befriend superstition; in short, they present themselves tangibly by both volatility and stability. This broad sameness through cultural orientation in public education[12] and by social media depicts an enduring future for the West, populous and diverse, that with integrative zest aborts repressive blemishes and promotes goodness.[13] Western likemindedness and fair-mindedness improvise bonds of unity the better to contain its citizens until none, ideally, not even the homeless, live outside the social margins.[14]

Because of this homogenous spirit, Westerners despise destructive urges—for example: the idolatries of Nazism/Fascism,[15] racism,[16] xenophobia, and communism[17]—that immobilize the overall moral lines for its sense

---

11. Hedges, *America*, 27, "When a government watches you twenty-four hours a day you cannot use the word 'liberty.' This is the relationship between a master and a slave."

12. Saul, *The Unconscious Civilization*, 68, "The existence of high-quality national public education school systems for the first dozen or so years of training is the key to a democracy where legitimacy lies with the citizens."

13. Contrarian: Ferguson. *Civilization*, 17–18, " . . . Western civilization appears to have lost confidence in itself."

14. Harpur, *God Help Us*, 17, " . . . it's a scandal of well-nigh cosmic proportions that in a world where some enjoy so much, many millions go to sleep every night starving, sick, homeless, or afraid for their very lives."

15. Steyn, *Lights Out*, 176, "Fascism ... had many takers in those parts of the cultural west that were politically deficient—ie, continental Europe—but it had minimal support in the heart of the political west—ie, the English-speaking world."

16. Toynbee, *Civilization On Trial*, 10, "Race and environment were the two main rival keys that were offered by would-be scientific nineteenth-century Western historians for solving the problem of cultural inequality of various extant human societies, and neither key proved, on trial, to unlock the fast-closed door."

17. Mishra, *Bland Fanatics*, 1–2, "For [Reinhold Niebuhr], the bigger culprits of history were, of course, communists and fascists. A dedicated anti-communist, the American theologian was vulnerable to phrases such as 'the moral superiority of Western civilization'. Nevertheless, he could see the peculiar trajectory of liberalism: how 'a dogma which was intended to guarantee the economic freedom of the individual became the "ideology" of vast corporate structures of a later period of capitalism, used by them,

of righteousness. Such prudent warring for Westernism generates high self-esteem and nourishes congenial ideals of self-righteous generosity.[18]

\/

The West's prevailing religiosity, humanism,[19] takes captive every thought in order that its utopian spirit own the ages. Westerners thus think for themselves within the limits of physical, psychological, political, social, and economic sciences with rational goals in mind, as self-discovery, self-realization, self-pleasuring, and self-glorying.

> Humanism constitutes a philosophical school that rejects all divinity and replaces the Divinity and every other divinity with human autonomy for ruling the earth and the heavens, which autonomy presupposes both the goodness and the capability for resolving complications while offering human fulfillment.[20] In its Western neo-liberalism format, humanism controls living reality.[21]

---

and still used, to prevent a proper political control of their power."

Dreher, *Live Not By Lies*, xiii, " . . . communism was militantly atheistic and declared religion to be its mortal enemy."

Morgan, *Australia*, 94, " . . . to support underdeveloped countries in south-east Asia to improve their living standards and access to technology as a means of staving off the lure of Communism."

18. Fukuyama, *Identity*, 10, "Self-esteem arises out of esteem by others."

19. Harari, *Homo Deus*, 259, "The humanist religion worships humanity, and expects humanity to play the part that God played in Christianity and Islam, and that the laws of nature played in Buddhism and Daoism." 275, "Humanism assumes that each human has a single authentic inner self, but when I try to attend to it I often encounter either silence or a cacophony of contending voices."

20. Hazard, *The European Mind*, xviii, 1680–1715 became . . . "a tribunal before which Man himself is arraigned in order that he may declare whether he was born innocent or stained with sin; whether his hopes of happiness were centred mainly on this world, or on the world to come; ideas so pregnant with life, so rich in power whether for attack or defence, that even now the force of that movement is far from spent, so far, indeed, that when to-day we deal with our present problems—religious, philosophical, political, social—we are but continuing in a measure the great and unresolved disputes of an earlier day."

21. Packer and Howard, *Christianity*, 16, "The secular humanism that we meet today is not the same thing as the Renaissance humanism which one sees in such men as Erasmus and Leonardo da Vinci. (Renaissance humanism, despite some murky streaks, was in essence a plea for a rich and robust Christian culture.) Nor should we equate secular humanism with the humanism professed by those who teach the humanities professionally; nor should we confuse it with the spirit of sympathetic concern for others' welfare which is often called humanism in these days."

The pleasure of this worshiping is that it showers spurious favors as wealth and power on sycophants.[22] Subsequently, Western civilization vibrates energetically, perpetually flinching at the fearful thought that the Christ will in the coming Judgment run the whole of this civilization over the edge into damnation and forever destroy its idolatrous existence.

ASSIMILATIVE THOUGHTS

Every civilization comes into existence by historical development, a continuation of rising and falling and rising.[23] Western civilization from the twentieth century sliding into and through the twenty-first runs amidst insecurities on an aggressive philosophical arc designed to shackle humanity within the here and now. Its gods and goddesses repel other, more secure religiosities as hostile and irrational, contrary to human wellbeing.[24]

\/

---

22. Huntington, *The Clash of Civilizations*, 104, "Wealth, like power, is assumed to be proof of virtue, a demonstration of moral and cultural superiority."

23. Oswald Spengler in *The Decline of the West* (1918–1922) followed a fatalistic pattern, its ending doom-laden and sad.

Arnold Toynbee's *A Study of History* (1936–1954) followed cycles of challenge, response, and decline. Decline occurs when timorous leaders fail to answer debilitating challenges.

Toynbee, *Civilization On Trial*, 12, "*Pace* Spengler, there seems to be no reason why a succession of stimulating challenges should not be met by a succession of victorious responses *ad infinitum*." 15, "While civilizations rise and fall and, in falling, give rise to others, some purposeful enterprise, higher than theirs, may at all times be making headway, and, in a divine plan, the learning that comes through the suffering caused by the failures of civilizations may be the sovereign means of progress."

Huntington, *The Clash of Civilizations*, 44:

For Pitrim Sorokin civilizations pass through ideational, sensate, and idealistic phases, typically Hegelian.

Carroll Quigley's patterning for civilization passes through seven stages: mixture, gestation, expansion, conflict, universal empire, decay, and invasion.

Hedges, *America*, 22, "Civilizations over the past six thousand years have the habit of eventually squandering their futures through acts of colossal stupidity and hubris."

Each thinker conforms history to a deterministic/fatalistic doom.

24. Packer and Howard, *Christianity*, 17, "The thought is that only those who know they are on their own in the universe, with no God to worship and no concern about the church, will ever take the bold steps that are needed to set their lives straight."

The more you find yourselves identifying with the spirit of the West rather than the Christ's teachings in the Church for the revelation of the Kingdom, the more imperative the summons to self-examination.

Assimilation, blending into the surrounding secularizing culture, happens *naturally*, without pain, except perhaps now and then a twinge of conscience. Rather, this accommodation—world conformity—makes the pain of being different from the broader community less, and less, painful, like sliding down a quiet river in a rubber raft. Each congregation drifting into the Western heart ignores the hypocrisy for easing into pain-free territory while at the same time upholding the historic statements of faith. Gliding into enculturation occurs almost irresistibly.

The West with its many values, norms, institutions, and behaviors drawn from Christianity bulks large as a satanic angel of light. Its *charm* tempts the unwary who fall for look-alike duplicity and follow reprobates into the Pit.

In the West HORIZONTALLY

ON THE HORIZONTAL LEVEL the West moves through unstable realities, geographical and demographical upheavals and collapses, each jarring loose immeasurable anxieties. These disturbances and disruptions—migratory movements, extreme weather patterns, natural disasters, rising sea levels,[1] urban constructions, agricultural shortages, pandemics,[2] and political confrontations—dislocate as well as destroy familiar perspectives; each tears away at civilizational strengths. The West, compact as shifting sands, constantly undergoes unprecedented dislocations, physically as well as socially.[3]

Migratory Movements

The West draws migrants by the thousands,[4] in the past by the millions. As immigrants enter through front doors of government offices or as refugees walk over unmanned border crossings, they escape meteorological,[5] eco-

---

1. McKibben, *Falter*, 34–35, "... the added weight of the new sea-water starts to bend the earth's crust."

2. Pains of the traumatic 1918 Spanish Flu still reverberate. See: Arnold, *Pandemic 1918* and Spinney, *Pale Rider*.

3. Harari, *Homo Deus*, 85, "For *Homo sapiens* has rewritten the rules of the game. This single apes species has managed within 70,000 years to change the global ecosystem in radical and unprecedented ways. Our impact is already on a par with that of the ice ages and tectonic movements."
 Jones, *Darwin's Ghost*, 55, "... the existence of any creature is a constantan struggle against relentless foes."

4. Jones, *Darwin's Ghost*, 56, "Most migrants share a history of repeated disaster by many and dramatic success by a few."

5. Oreskes and Conway, *The Collapse of Western Civilization*, 30, "Analysts had predicted that an eight-meter sea level rise would dislocate 10 percent of the global population. Alas, their estimates proved low; the reality was closer to 20 percent. Although

nomic, racial, and political crises to enter into *irresistible* electro-magnetic attractions of freedom, wealth, and safety that the West represents. Escapees from rising sea levels, generational poverty, economic stagnation, ethnic hatreds, and political reprisals arrive from Africa, South America, Central America, the Middle East, and Asia often after perilous trekking over land and/or by sea. These peoples through governmental assistance programs change the demographic face of the West, Europe, for instance, into a possible Eurabia.[6]

Social movements occur also internally, individuals and families leaving agricultural areas for more advantageous living conditions in cities; these Westerners find the lure of urban and suburban futures too strong to resist, even if it means at first surviving in inner-city enclaves of immigrant minorities.

Current influxes and fluxes of population movements also include migrant workers who, augmenting income, stoop to menial labor that unwilling Westerners refuse. These farm workers, nannies, and nursing-home employees willingly toil long hours in exhausting jobs to participate in and benefit from Western materialism.

Year after year foreign students register with Western universities and colleges to take advantage of the *status* that these institutions confer and the travel experiences that enrich personal strengths. Many of these newcomers

---

records for this period are incomplete, it is likely that during the Mass Migration 1.5 billion people were displaced around the globe, either directly from the impacts of sea level rise or indirectly from other impacts of climate change, including the secondary dislocation of inland peoples whose towns and villages were overrun by eustatic refugees."

Oreskes and Conway's historical and futuristic essay perceives the West from the perspective of AD 2093.

McKibben, *Falter*, 34, "In 2015 a study in the *Journal of Mathematical Biology* pointed out that if the world's oceans kept warming, by 2100 they might become hot enough to 'stop oxygen production by phytoplankton by disrupting the process of photosynthesis. Given that two-thirds of the earth's oxygen comes from phytoplankton, that would 'likely result in the mass mortality of animals and humans.'"

6. To offset fears of an Eurabia: Mishra, *Bland Fanatics*, 32, "So what if Muslims account for only 3 to 4 per cent of the EU's total population of 493 million?" 41–42, "For many of these Muslim aspirants for full and equal citizenship, the urgent questions are whether the old-style liberalism of many European nation states, which has traditionally assumed cultural homogeneity, can accommodate minority identity, and whether majority communities in Europe can tolerate expressions of cultural and religious distinctiveness."

seek immigrant status to live and work in constellations of hope well-nigh impossible in countries of origin.[7]

All in all, Western populations[8] shift and swing, which alterations occupy demographers and census-takers; these statisticians graphically enumerate the relentless strains upon cities and towns, governments and NGOs, also teachers and welfare workers. Throughout, race-baiters find ready victims among migrants.[9]

\/

Immigrants alter the West's racial composition from the surface tranquility of *presumed* monochromatic Caucasian white to a more brownish blend.[10] First, refugee families have higher birthrates, thereby altering Western racial alignments.[11] Second, through intermarrying—miscegenation legally aborted—immigrants and refugees mix with whites and whites with refugees and immigrants; children of mixed marriages now represent the slow birthing of a multi-racial homogeneity, central to which a population unity hitherto considered impossible. Slowly intermarrying old/white with new/colored unites the West into a United Nations' permanent tan.

Within immigrant communities tensions contribute to overall restlessness. Adults struggle daily with the risks for children through assimilation and integration.[12] Do they now obey the cultural expectations of

---

7. Toynbee, *Civilization On Trial*, 82–83, " . . . a younger generation of non-Westerners from all the once-separate societies which the West has now swept together in its world-enveloping net has literally been coming to school in the West in our day."

8. Social classes constantly disappear and reappear, changing national compositions.
Boyd, *Canadian Law*, 12, " . . . dialectical materialism, must lead to the violent overthrow of the capitalist class . . . .. Events would then progress toward the ideal of a classless society."

9. Huntington, *The Clash of Civilizations*, 42, "The crucial distinctions among human groups concern their values, beliefs, institutions, and social structures, not their physical size, head shapes, and skin colors."

10. Ferguson, *Civilization*, 138–139, " . . . American society is also becoming racially blended as never before. The US census distinguishes between four 'racial' categories: 'black', 'white', 'North American', and 'Asian or Pacific Islander'. On this basis, one in every twenty children in the United States is of mixed origin, in that their parents do not belong to the same racial category."

11. Du Bois, *The Soul of Black Folks*, 62, "Hence arises a new human unity, pulling the ends of the earth nearer, and all men, black, yellow, and white."

12. Fukuyama, *Identity*, 68, "Like many children of immigrants, they are eager to distance themselves from their families' old-fashioned ways of life."

countries left behind or integrate into xenophobic neighboring communities? Capacities for learning to live within Western anticipations pressure immigrant communities to experience and next generations to participate in strengths as well as angsts of this larger civilization.

Westerners with old ancestries now merge with migrant peoples who seek an accepting welcome.[13] Whatever Caucasian vacillation, right-wing resistance, and further victimization, the different colors may resolve into one distinctive race or kill each other in brutally bloody civil wars.

Inarguably, enormous population movements alter unalterably the whole of Western demographics; this social acceptance of others nullifies every effort at racial repose in one color or another, and diminishes every manifestation of racial pride.[14]

Weather Extremes

Wasting heat waves[15] and wretched monster storms,[16] by degrees deadlier hurricanes, tornados, cyclones, typhoons, and, unforgettably, bewildering fire behaviors, damage ecosystems and break human lives. As evidence of climate change ruinous droughts and crop failures afflict the West with mutilating tensions, disfiguring stresses, and even biophobia.[17] These calamities, with social disintegrations and environmental costs, open up inevitable chain reactions, breaking down transport systems and emptying store shelves.

---

13. Morgan, *Australia*, 25, "There was also a general view that the racial horrors of the Second World War should lead to a greater connection between ethnic, linguistic, and racial groups in the post-war world."

14. Mishra, B*land Fanatics*, 49-50, "Racism was—and is—more than an ugly prejudice, something to be eradicated through legal and social proscription."

15. Morgan, *Australia*, 3, "The last ten years, in fact, have been Australia's warmest decade on record."

McKibben, *Falter*, 48, "The Great Barrier Reef is the largest living structure on Earth, but it is roughly half as living as it was three years ago."

16. Winchester, *Pacific*, 236, "The storms created in this ocean are coming to be recognized as the harbingers of the weather in the rest of the planet—the very first indicators of, maybe even the generators of, the swirls of wind, pressure, and humidity that sweep from the west to east as the world turns beneath them."

17. Thunberg, *No One Is Too Small To Make a Difference*, 12-13, "[Politicians] only talk about moving forward with the same bad ideas that got us into this mess."

As meteorologists algorithmically project more weather extremes, they wishfully seek understanding of present cataclysms, while displaced peoples struggle for elemental water, food, shelter, and breathing space.

Urban Immensities

Across the West metropolitan growth grapples with aggressive industrial demands to satisfy insatiable needs for human accommodation. For more construction sites builders ruin irreplaceable agricultural spaces and sully invaluable wetlands. Opening more four-lane highways between cities and towns also consumes thousands upon thousands of hectares better suitable for agrarian usage and wildlife conservancy. Urbanization by massing populations savages the purposes of open spaces, catastrophically. Poor urban and suburban planning buries under tarmac many necessities for life, human as well as animal. Affinities for misjudging the worth of farmlands and the wellsprings of life in forests, woodlots, wetlands, and neighborhood gardens slowly abuse the vitals of Western civilization. As population concentrations and industrial parklands disfigure the face of the West, demonstrable damages to prime agricultural and green spaces proliferate.

While inner cities decay, urban planners reach beyond population centers and green belts to appease the hungers of builders, house-hunters, and high-rise dwellers for more and more asphalt-defiled habitats. Cries of protest only add to already vociferous noise pollutions and drift past hearing-impaired city fathers/mothers.

Immigrants populating the West do more than offset failing Caucasian birthrates; they encourage urban growth. Now bourgeoning cities large and small oblige consumer societies readily and willingly to break protective greenbelt legislation, if the price is right and the political wandering away from conservation commitments tempting enough. The testiness of this predicament attains to more messy socio-political hazards, radical voting blocs squaring off.

Agricultural Casualties

As misaligned metropolitan planning commissions make farmland vanish, never to resurface, the industrial and housing urgencies conceal under *civilization* crucial agricultural lands—meter by meter or yard by yard. These shrinking Australasian, Northern European, and North American breadbaskets necessitate more dependencies for food on sources abroad. Loss of agricultural spaces—pasture and crop lands—limit notions of limitless food sources. Whereas once sweeping forests and undulating plains dominated horizons with promises of sufficient food stuffs for uncountable populations, now encroaching human habitations with huge waste spaces rebuff the potentials of once awesome public resources.

Large-scale farming, genetic engineering, and hydroponics may modify immediate famine dangers,[18] yet dystopic visions hover over irreplaceable rural lands to encourage hoarding of necessities and provoke seething feuds between the haves and the have-nots.[19]

Manufacturing Revolutions

The West prospers as a consumer society,[20] the whole energized by the manufacturing industry. Since the Industrial Revolution that started approximately in the second half of the eighteenth century factories produce goods saleable also in rural areas[21] and to people in the faraway. Once billowing smokestacks dominated the skylines of cities and town—signs of

---

18. McKibben, *Falter*, 36, "We've had an amazing run since the end of World War II, with crop yields growing fast enough to keep ahead of a fast-rising population. It's come at great human cost—displaced peasant farmers fill many of the planet's vast slums—but in terms of sheer volume, the Green Revolution's fertilizers, pesticides, and machinery managed to push output sharply upward. That climb, however, now seems to be running into the brute facts of heat and drought."
Greenspan, *The Age of Turbulence*, 253, quoting one Amartya Sen, "In the terrible history of famines in the world, no substantial famine has ever occurred in any independent and democratic country with a relatively free press."
Ferguson, *Doom*, 179.

19. Harari, *Homo Deus*, 64, "Even if famine, plague and war become less prevalent, billions of humans in developing countries and seedy neighbourhoods will continue to deal with poverty, illness and violence even as the elites are already reaching for eternal youth and godlike powers."

20. Hedges, *America*, 232, "The message of the consumer society, pumped out over flat screen televisions, computers, and smartphones to those trapped at the bottom of society is shrill and unrelenting: *You are a failure*. Popular culture celebrates those who wallow in power, wealth, and self-obsession, and perpetuates the lie that if you work hard and are clever, you can become a 'success,' perhaps landing on *American Idol* or *Shark Tank*."

21. Ferguson, *Civilization*, 198, "The consumer society is so all-pervasive today that it is easy to assume it has always existed. Yet in reality it is one of the more recent innovations that propelled the West ahead of the Rest. Its most striking characteristic is its seemingly irresistible appeal."

prosperity and full employment—but now crumble on account of pollution controls. In place of cheap and dirty fossil fuels, electricity conforms factories to modern construction requirements without diminishing demands. Houses, vehicles, clothes, packaged foods, etc., spur industries to further revolutionize society and have people purchase more, endlessly more obsolescing merchandize. Huge demands for wasteful goods articulate Western racial superiority and cultural success, counting those with less and least as failures. Such mean-mindedness identifies the sanctimonious spirit of the West. To satisfy the cravings for cheaper products and more profits economic actors outsource manufacturing to Mexico, China, and other Asian countries, leaving worrisome unemployment behind.

Due to Western covetousness, aristocratic overlords manufacturing unnecessary goods contribute to higher and more expansive landfill sites. These heaps of bygone values and valuables now require continuous costly maintenance and expensive monitoring to prevent air, water, and soil pollutions from poisoning surrounding communities.

Surface Wreckages

Catastrophic fires, denuded forests, melting glaciers,[22] tidal waves, killer floods, ominously rising sea levels, life-shattering earthquakes, and erupting volcanoes afflict the West; each natural disaster wrecks human communities and wildlife ecosystems, sending refugees scrambling for shelter and hospitality in the elsewhere. As arbitrary death strikes in an indeterministic manner, it dehumanizes habitats and desolates societies; loss of life more than degrades the surface of the West. These natural disasters destroy, leaving grief-stricken survivors toiling amidst the damages.

Instability on the earth's surface, rock-solid upon initial encounter, disturbs every placid assumption and disrupts every flight of fancy seeking a sure foundation. Take the 2019–2022 novel-coronavirus pandemic.[23] Sneaking out of a hidden spot, possible in the Far East, the wildly-spreading virus with its variants imposed upon the West numerous deaths, left behind

---

22. McKibben, *Falter*, 34, "Or consider this: as ice sheets melt, they take weight of land, and that can trigger earthquakes—seismic activity is already increasing in Greenland and Alaska."

23. Ferguson, *Doom*, 5, "A pandemic is made up of a new pathogen and the social networks that it attacks."

many broken bodies,[24] altered communications, and shook communities to the core. As this malignity spread destruction and death, it unleashed waves of anxiety, tension, and stress, stretched health care systems, brought about on-line educational structures, and disturbed psyches that require decades of psychological/emotional healing. Old and young marked by this unprecedented calamity, at least since the post-First World War Spanish Flu, contributed to opioid addictions, alcoholic delusions, broken marriages, disrupted families, and children afraid to socialize. Hence, the damaging powers of natural disasters in the air, on the ground, and under the surface enlarge the evidence of visible wreckages, which impair confidence in the physical soundness of this civilization.[25]

Surface destructions, some less visible initially than others, plague the West and push this civilization floundering toward the vexing edge, fearing the unpredictability of natural disasters. Unpreparedness for devastations settles depressive clouds over the land and drives trauma into psyches, the more perceptive the first to recoil emotionally and mentally.

Political Disappointments

Conservative and liberal/socialist legislators naively chosen by Western voters compete with respective platforms to govern in the midst of unstable realities. Each type of government proposes its critical platforms to alleviate, if possible contain, incomputable causes of the instabilities as well as follies of the age. With unpredictable talents for compromise they set aside the truth of political convictions for meeting places to the left or to the right, or in between.[26] Contrary to whatever the political promises, rival factions of parliamentarian law-makers and law-keepers now with soft totalitarian appeal lessen at best human dysfunctionalities, most frequently only by throwing money at vocalized pains. This leaves good Westerners

---

24. Ferguson, *Doom*, 4, "... the cumulative body count continues to rise globally at a rate of more than 3:5 percent a week—to say nothing of the number of people whose health has been permanently damaged, which no one yet has yet estimated."

25. Harari, *Homo Deus*, 85, "Some people fear that today we are again in mortal danger of massive volcanic eruptions or colliding asteroids."

26. The political left is often associated with nationalization of industry, increased public spending, trade union power, and unilateral disarmament, trademarks of socialism.
Fukuyama, *Identity*, 76, "... parties of the left are nowhere the dominant forces they were through the late twentieth century."

SELF-EXAMINATION

fretting amidst living priorities of clearing up wreckages left by pandemic, wind, water, and fire. The whole of political processes frequently serves as an elite sport carried out to please voters' limited participation. Political figures raise hopes. Circumstances dash hopes. Throughout however people, irreducibly arbitrary, do interfere with even the best of political expectations that assure relief from forces breaking up the surface of the West.

As groundbreaking alterations trouble the West, all government-founded and financed institutions—the United Nations, the North American Treaty Organization, the International Labor Organization, the European Union,[27] the International Monetary Fund, the European Central Bank, the World Bank, North American Aerospace Defense Command, the Southeast Asia Treaty Organization, the Collective Security Treaty Organization, ANZUS, the British Commonwealth, the Strategic Defense Initiative, the Atlantic Charter, the World Trade Organization, G-7 groupings, G-20 alignments, etc.—as well as military maneuverings by land, sea, and air, fail to halt even temporarily the extensive and painful alterations troubling the horizontal face of Western civilization's features.

With China economically and militarily moving to replace America as the powerhouse of the world,[28] with Russia militarily expanding into the West,[29] into the Crimea and the Ukraine for now, with India demanding recognition on the world stage, with Iran hungering to own the Middle East, and with rogue revolutionary powers holding nuclear weapons capable of mutually assured destruction and global annihilation, these rival organizations, each in its own way, seek out the West's jugular, while Western politicians wander and waver before imponderables that trouble the whole people of the West.

---

27. Ferguson, *The Great Degeneration*, 13, Britain/England through the Brexit maneuver broke with the European Union because bureaucrats in Brussels, Belgium encroached on and frittered away the British sense of freedom.

28. Morgan, *Australia*, 95, "Australia's interest in creating a defensive buffer zone between China and its own shores was further boosted in 1954 with the signing of the South-East Asia Collective Defence Treaty under the auspices of SEATO (the South-East Asia Treaty Organization)."

29. Thatcher, *The Downing Street Years*, 156, "The Soviet Union was increasingly arrogant; the Third World was increasingly aggressive in its demands for international redistribution of wealth; the West is increasingly apt to quarrel with itself, and to cut special deals with bodies like OPEC." 238, " . . . from its foundation in May 1955 the Warsaw Pact was always an instrument of Soviet power."

IN THE WEST HORIZONTALLY

ASSIMILATIVE THOUGHTS

Migratory movements, weather extremes, urban immensities, agricultural casualties, manufacturing revolutions, surface wreckages, and political disappointments incontestably modify and scar Western civilization, leaving human communities distraught, unable to comprehend the intensities of altering situations. None of the dire times and asymmetric happenings may be shrugged off, and never the precariousness of human life. Skeptics may seek hiding places in forgetfulness, compile conspiracies, assume they will outlast the worst, or pretend that the troubles will never confront them personally. Unable even to prevent the common cold, huge majorities may fatalistically shoulder what will be, will be, to leave multi-dimensional generations suffering worse. Aristocrats may rely on the deceitfulness of wealth to escape calamity. Scientists may rise above the devastations and contradictions with evolutionary hopes of a bionic race living even beyond the Moon, on Mars, on Saturn's Titan, or on an even more remote asteroid for mining purposes.[30] For all others one fact stands fast: Westerners going over to the foremost edge undergo portentous insecurities; all lack of confidence aggravates worsening deprivations.

Consider: are you pained by cultural shifts, population movements, social dislocations, and ground-level scythes of death? Or do you, boosted by arrogance or cowering under piles of cash, not care?

Under all circumstances, inconveniently, the Lord Jesus calls his own burdened by these existential fears to immediate self-examination, thereby to prove the sovereignty of grace, the eternal solidity of the Kingdom, as well as the looming end of reprobation.

---

30. Hedges, *America*, 260, "We have no other place to go. Earth is my home. Do not be fearful of change. Out of the chaos comes balance and harmony. There really is a need for us to reevaluate that relationship we have with Mother Earth."

In the West VERTICALLY

The class-conscious West divides simply. The Top Tier exhales Western happiness and the Bottom Tier inhales Western happiness, thereby participating in the perceived contentment with wealth that the Top Tier exudes. Top-Tier people export genius in happiness. Bottom-Tier people with different rates of success import Top-Tier gratifications with wealth. Bottom-Tier citizens calculate the benefits of and appreciate the satisfactions wafting down from the Top Tier, thus inspiring lower-class souls also to luxuriate in the deep confusions associated with the making of and trusting in money.[1]

It must be said, the Christ looks unsympathetically at core covetousness, mammonism[2] over which he placed an indisputable curse.

- First Timothy 6:9–10, "... those who desire to be rich fall into temptation, into a snare, into many senseless and harmful desires that plunge people into ruin and destruction. For the love of money is a root of all kinds of evils. It is through this craving that some have wandered away from the faith and pierced themselves with many pangs."
- Hebrews 13:5p, "Keep your life free from love of money."
- Psalm 73:16–17, "But when I thought to understand [the covetous], it seemed to be a wearisome task, until I went into the sanctuary of God: then I discerned their end."

The Lord Jesus through the Scriptures revealed the condemnation he placed upon greediness until now every Bible-reading Westerner finds no worthwhile excuse for mammonism in the moment the Christ calls each

---

1. Harari, *Homo Deus*, 168, "Money ... has no objective value. You cannot eat, drink or wear a dollar bill. Yet as long as billions of people believe in its value, you can use it to buy food, beverages and clothing."
2. Matthew 6:24.

to stand before him and receive the judgment he handed down from Golgotha, Hebrews 9:27. As you find yourselves taking on Western idolatrous living as normal and comforting now is the hour of self-examination.

TOP TIER DYNAMICS

At the pyramidal zenith of Western happiness, the Top Tier, reigns humanism, typically idolic. Its deities have improved on past idolatries that were the works of human hands, thus neither able to see, hear, or speak. Top-Tier idol-figures do see, hear, and speak. They are the sports idols, the movie stars, and the financial tycoons/magnates selfishly needful of admiration and adulation. Collectively, the community of the stars is physically beautiful and/or unbelievably rich, mirrored in sport tabloids, fashion magazines, and on financial pages—a star-studded, photogenic, and economically powerful host of aloof multi-millionaires and multi-billionaires that as the precarious powers of the age do as they please.[3] These, the high-standing aristocrats of the West, cosmopolitans and internationalists, together symbolize the happiness found in wealth and champion ascendancy into money-heaven.[4] Given the apotheosis of Top-Tier residents Bottom-Tier

---

3. Thunberg, *No One Is Too Small To Make a Difference*, 41, "People see you celebrities as gods. You influence billions of people."

McKibben, *Falter*, 15, " . . . much of this book will be devoted to examining the godlike powers that come with our rapid increases in computing speed, everything from human genetic engineering to artificial intelligence."

Campbell, *The Masks of God*, 21, "A god can be simultaneously in two or more places—like a melody, or like the form of a traditional mask. And wherever he comes, the impact of his presence is the same: it is not reduced through multiplication."

4. Ferguson, *The Great Degeneration*, 4, "Throughout the English-speaking world, the income share of the top '1 per cent' of households has risen since around 1980. The same thing has happened, albeit to a lesser extent in some European states, notably Finland, Norway and Portugal, as well as in many emerging markets, including China."

Thunberg, *No One Is Too Small To Make a Difference*, 13, "We are about to sacrifice our civilization for the opportunity of a very small number of people who continue to make enormous amounts of money. We are about to sacrifice the biosphere so that rich people in the countries like mine can live in luxury. But it is the suffering of the many which pay for the luxuries of the few." 20, "Here in Davos—just like everywhere else—everyone is talking about money. It seems that money and growth are our only main concerns."

McKibben, *Falter*, 117, "The Gilded Age robber barons (or, if you prefer, the captains of industry) pushed wealth, and hence political power, as sharply their way in the late nineteenth century as have the libertarian billionaires of our time."

Boyd, *Canadian Law*, 19, "The central idea of libertarianism is that people should be permitted to run their own lives as they wish."

commoners listen to star-talk and look up hopefully, even prayerfully, for similar successes.

Top Tier Allure

By denying the existence of divine beings, postmodern Westerners learn to do as they please; in so doing they make themselves into little gods,[5] defining thereby a dominant feature of Postmodernism. People who do as they please self-idolize. This self-idolization is one aspect of absolute autonomy.

Or, to find better stability amidst these unstable idolizing realities, more likely Westerners apotheosize others, unaccountable main gods, the pantheon of Top-Tier makers and shakers—film stars, sport idols, and financial tycoons. These Hollywood glitterati,[6] sport heroes, and corporate bosses rule the West. Typical of all elusive features of the religiosities, Top-Tier gods—gods hitherto unknown—little tolerate other divinities to encroach on their territory and invade their domesticated preserve. To live in the West Bottom-Tier people therefore become like them, in money lust.[7]

Top-Tier god-like creatures in pantheonic settings maintain courts of power by stimulating cupidity in worshipers' hearts; Western people naturally believe this money-credo. As the advertisements of Top-Tier happiness flash through Bottom-Tier multi-media, millionaires and billionaires brag they have arrived and happily made good. These moneyed gods now hire Bottom-Tier money managers to bank bourgeoning monetary

---

5. Harari, *Homo Deus*, 49, "In seeking bliss and immortality humans are in fact trying to upgrade themselves into gods. Not just because these are divine qualities, but because in order to overcome old age and misery humans will first have to acquire godlike control of their own biological substratum." 50, "The upgrading of humans into gods may follow any of three paths: biological engineering, cyborg engineering and the engineering of non-organic beings." 53, "In the twenty-first century, the . . . big project of humankind will be to acquire for us divine powers of creation and destruction, and upgrade *Homo sapiens* into *Homo Deus*."

6. Shapiro, *The Authoritarian Moment*, 140, " . . . Hollywood has long dedicated itself to the simple proposition that prestige pictures must fulfill leftist messaging requirements, and moneymakers must please the public."

Shapiro, 6, *Primetime Propaganda*, 6, "Hollywood, with its godlike powers, has succeeded far beyond its wildest dreams, shaping America's styles, tastes, politics, and even family structures." 15, " . . . the gods retain a considerable advantage in resources and talent."

7. Psalm 135:18, "Those who make [idols] become like them, so do all who trust in them."

gains[8] and simultaneously show blinkered Bottom-Tier classes how to live. Throughout the West, active hotbed of humanism,[9] the deities of this day display through relevant commercials opulent abundance and the irresistible happiness that money buys.[10]

While affluent aristocrats at ease in overflowing happiness display the advantages of success, they also play one-upmanship in the opaque community of the gods. The richer find they are mightier, more ably bending political ears to craft beneficial legislation.[11] Thus they embellish much-repeated satisfaction that powers of money buy. As the Top-Tier social hierarchy in its distant heavens displays expressions of contentment, these liberal-minded gods motivate Bottom-Tier Westerners to embrace similar goals, always persuading the lower classes to pay for Top-Tier's physical and emotional satisfactions.

Bottom-Tier people, to maintain the awe of this religiosity and bolster respect for the patriarchal/matriarchal authority of wealth, purchase numerous movie tickets and uncountable sports passes, along with identifying paraphernalia—jerseys, cups, caps, clothing, perfumes; etc.—therewith to flash personal connections to the passing gods. At the same time the voices of these gods and goddesses encourage Bottom-Tier populations to buy tycoons' products and services,[12] thus displaying connectedness to the only solid feature and valid cause now possible in the West, the more of which the better.

\/

---

8. Saul, *The Unconscious Civilization*, 15, " . . . our elite is primarily and increasingly managerial. A managerial elite manages. A crisis, unfortunately requires thought. Thought is not a management function."

9. Packer and Howard, *Christianity*, 17, "The heart of secular humanism . . . appears as reaction—reaction born, as it seems, of hurt and resentment, outrage and disgust at the tenets and track record of organized religion."

10. Hedges, *America*, 232, "The disparity between the glittering world that people watch and the bleak world they inhabit creates a collective schizophrenia. It manifests itself in diseases of despair—suicides, addictions, mass shootings, hate crimes, and depression, We are to blame for our own misfortune."

11. Thunberg, *No One Is Too Small To Make a Difference*, 18, "At places like Davos, people like to tell success stories. But their financial success has come with an unthinkable price-tag."

12. Saul, *The Unconscious Civilization*, 15, " . . . the income of the elites at the upper levels has continued to grow and at the middle levels has not declined."

Self-Examination

Western polytheism imbues impressionable multitudes across this mighty civilization with a powerful religiosity to imprison everyone within the tyranny of the dollar, or euro. Every Westerner now is a miniature god or a mini-goddess or, failing to earn the millions and billions necessary for divinity, worshipers of insouciant Top-Tier aristocrats dream of palatial homes, exotic vacations, private jets, and lavish lifestyles. From the lofty and cloudy regions of the Top Tier, Westerners manufacture a basic conviction that financial success rolls over onto the crest of happiness. As worshipers of mighty gods and goddesses, Westerners inspire each other to find the contentment granted in the greatest possible riches.[13] Hence all good citizens in the throes of polytheism strive to better themselves economically by greedy-in-gain believing that all who abide by the code of the West and simultaneously apply its work ethic can be millionaires and billionaires,[14] with lesser human beings left suffering poverty. Westerners hence follow a powerful polytheistic religion delightfully or desperately confirmed in the sensuality and materiality the many gods and goddesses have on display.

The above composite set of inspirational facts breeds unity in diversity; all in the community of the dollar, or euro, and all fired up by mammon-religiosity standardize the heart of the West.[15]

Top Tier Philosophy

By way of the fifteenth-sixteenth century Renaissance the West as a living entity broke out from under the papal tyranny of the Middle Ages and initiated its liberty in rationalist autonomy.[16] This autonomy came with

---

13. Confided the working-class single mother to her children at approaching on foot the local food bank, "You can be whatever you want to be."

14. Hedges, *America*, 243, "It is a culture based on self-absorption, medical procedures to mask aging, and narcissism. Any form of suffering, which is always part of self-sacrifice, is to be avoided. The plight of our neighbor is irrelevant."

15. A comparison: Dreher, *Live Not by Lies*, 23, "Russia's intellectual and creative classes fell under the sway of Prometheanism, the belief that man has unlimited godlike powers to make the world to suit his desires."

16. Hazard, *The European Mind*, xv, "Never was there a greater contrast, never a more sudden transition than this! An hierarchical system ensured by authority; life firmly based on dogmatic principle—such were the things held dear by the people of the seventeenth century; but these—controls, authority, dogmas, and the like—were the very things that their immediate successors of the eighteenth held in cordial detestation. The former were upholders of [Roman Catholicism]; the latter were its foes. The former believed in the laws of God; the latter in the laws of Nature; the former lived contentedly

two distinct foci, Emmanuel Kant's theology[17] and Isidore Marie Auguste François Xavier Comte's philosophy, the former more theoretical, the latter more practical. Each of these visionary complexities prepared the way for unprecedented Western covetousness. Shifting authority, from the popes to the people, started yearnings for the expediency of contentment in lavish wealth, wealth hitherto restricted to papal and political aristocracies of the Middle Ages.

Kant's Autonomy

Kant, 1724–1804, stood at the beginnings of Renaissance autonomy. Troubled by the competition between living humanity and unknowable gods, he closed off, shut away the distinction between the two major spheres known in the West, a bold strategy in boundless self-confidence. The one realm, the noumenal[18]—shadowy and beyond human comprehension—he restricted to the gods; on account of incomprehensibility these gods remained distant and silent, irrelevant to the dynamics of human living and ethics, hence maximally insignificant. The second realm, the phenomenal—rationally preferable and knowable—he peopled with autonomous beings capable of knowing themselves and the earth; he charged these suddenly proficient-in-autonomy leaders to rearrange in distinction from the Middle Ages the contemporary rules of life, the criterion for living, and the insights from developing sciences—astrology, anthropology, zoology; etc., thus to follow the science.[19]

---

enough in a world composed of unequal social grades; of the latter the one absorbing dream was Equality."

Packer and Howard, *Christianity*, 20, "Working hypotheses . . . which humanists embrace include the eternity and infinity of the universe; the evolution of man and society as a fact of the past and a hope for the future; the autonomy of man as lord of Nature, to do what he wants with it; the absolute uniformity of nature, according to the inherent laws of its functioning; utilitarian relativism in ethics, whereby anything that promises happy states and feelings becomes right for that very reason; and a belief that there should be shares for all in all good things."

17. Lindsell, *The New Paganism*, 75, "Along with Kant's denial of the propriety of metaphysics out went the notion of revelation."

18. Hazard, *The European Mind*, xvii, "The Divine was relegated to a vague and impenetrable heaven, somewhere up in the skies."

19. Jones, *Darwin's Ghost*, xxiii, ". . . and bitter as the disputes are, no scientist denies the central truth of *The Origin*, the idea of descent with modification." xviii, "The struggle for existence, the survival of the fittest and the origin of species are wisdom of the most

Self-Examination

In the Thomism of the waning Middle Ages quasi-supernatural Scholasticism ruled the West and revealed the goal in the ethics of life; dying Roman Catholicism postulated the death of the noumenal world. Westerners now freed from metaphysical interferences took strides in ordering primal societies in the humanist manner, according to its criteria of scientific observation and intellectual penetration of human nature. Without reliance on an external starting point, Renaissance man, of age, however much an abstraction, came alive and appropriated an autonomous canon with which to interpret the reality of the phenomenal real, apart from the now invalidated laws of the supernatural. Recoiling from perceived inconsistencies imposed by the noumenal realm, the Renaissance freed humanity from the supernatural as interpreted by Thomism. In the hour of liberation the shamefully exploitive constant of covetousness with indiscriminate zeal moved conclusively into the Western heart-ground of living.

With the noumenal sphere arbitrarily shut away, Western leadership at liberty from metaphysical interferences found prodigious freedom in autonomy, authority, and independence. This creation of early humanism vivified that self-determination that to this day differentiates Western reasoning ability from fatalistic regimes dominating mordant civilizations, the Mohammedan, Hindu, Buddhist, and others. Humanists now buoyed by the philosophy of the first Renaissance man, Kant, shoved abhorrent scholastic philosophies of the Middle Ages aside for visions in rational freedom, uninhibited by divine prohibitions. In that idealism the hugely competitive humanists broke open characteristic self-determination at reinterpreting and reorganizing nobler instincts to create through value judgments conformity in the new reality. By exercising the liberty of autonomous reason[20]—in an impactful manner saying: this is the world and the life we want—they eliminated every metaphysical referent to install in the West currently still functioning preferences. Hence, by way of Emmanuel Kant, Westerners through reason alone interpreted the natural world and in this world the nature of (human) life. Now with common currency men and women endeavor to create cultural and social interfaces that in each period of ensuing history surpasses the numinous dreams of empire-building Tower-of-Babel architects. Nature—now rationally accessible and

---

conventional kind."

20. Hazard, *The European Mind*, xvii, "Reason was no longer synonymous with sober good sense, with serene and benevolent wisdom. It became critical, aggressive. The most widely accepted notions, such as deriving proof of God's existence from universal consent, the historical basis of miracles, were openly called in question."

logically comprehensible—interpreted by sufficient means of reason gave in a continually changing West eventually one only constant, money, the persuasively dependable paradigm for fashionable talk and relentless acquisition.[21] Money ... is happiness.

Out of newfound freedom the humanists, perhaps at first naively, extracted a modern religiosity with unconditional authority sub-divided over millions and billions of god-like human beings or limited to a worshiped aristocracy of luminous gods and goddesses; Westerners rationalistically indoctrinated evolved to reject any interpretation of phenomenal reality that failed to advocate the freedom of earning money. This hypersensitive authority generated its own principles—the way, the life, and the truth—whereby to reshape Western civilization in its own image, the rise and evolution of which locked the West into a massive, massive mammon-spell. Renaissance freedom of reasoning initiated venturing into a new religiosity.[22]

Comte's Autonomy

Comte, 1798–1857, recharged the motor force of the Renaissance and assisted thereby the West's transition into the Enlightenment.[23] He raised the profligate ideal of human autonomy to superlative heights: total disengagement from any and all divine interference.[24] In his idealistic state of mind he planned the perfect Western civilization, the whole pulsing with the energies of liberty that scientific wisdom exalted. In the widening societal disparities between remnants of religiosity and the new age,

21. Packer and Howard, *Christianity*, 23, "Enlightenment humanism comes from men like Voltaire and Kant, children of the eighteenth-century rationalism which glorified cool reasoners; it has always prided itself on maintaining without Christian sanction a moral code equal if not superior to that of Christianity."

22. Hazard, *The European Mind*, xvi-xvii, "The champions of Reason and the champions of Religion were ... fighting desperately for the possession of men's souls, confronting each other in a contest at which the whole of thoughtful Europe was looking on."

23. Lindsell, *The New Paganism*, quoting one Peter Gay, 47, "The men of the Enlightenment united on a vastly ambitious program of secularism, humanity, cosmopolitanism, and freedom, above all, freedom in its many forms—freedom from arbitrary power, freedom of speech, freedom of trade, freedom to realize one's talents, freedom of aesthetic response, freedom, in a word, of moral man to make his own way in the world." Individualistically.

24. Hazard, *The European Mind*, xvii, "Man and man alone was the standard by which all things were measured."

Self-Examination

Comte, as an early Enlightenment personage, perceived a process in which François-Marie Arouet, alias Voltaire,[25] 1694–1778, had dominated. Presciently, Comte saw Western civilization transferring itself 1) out of the pre-scientific theological age of stagnation dominant in the Middle Ages, 2) through still enslaving metaphysical speculations, 3) into the bright light of the positivistic environment and age devoid of religious verifiers and above all free from reprehensible priestly truth-makers. In the first stage citizens yet embosomed biblical teachings as the basis for living; this applied to Christians as well as Roman Catholics and Jews. In the second phase, the metaphysical, Renaissance people still believed in a mosaic of eternal values as guides for societal living, values slowly dying in pools of isolation. And in the third, history's point of pride, the reign of scientific men (and women), everyone liberated from religious guidance as well as metaphysical restrictions. Comte, future-facing, perceived all evidence of religiosity rusting and rotting away on Western landfill sites. Obviously, this Enlightenment thrust moved far beyond Kant's phenomenal/noumenal distinction. Comte eliminated every reference to religiosity, above all the noumenal. No heaven covered this projected super-civilization.

Comte's sociologically aligned *progressivism* replaced the now antiquated scholastic hierarchy of the Middle Ages for a totally committed humanism, its self-acclaimed good people bound to an ethic of service for transforming first Western civilization. Liberation from the edicts of supernatural authorities for the forthcoming scientifically imbued community of citizens moving with matchless solidarity raised hopes humanistically high. In this community designed for prosperity Comte perceived a Western civilization structured solidly on the principle of human decency, the whole easing into a reality without national divisions,[26] its highly cosmopolitan world ahead of tides of depravity, a world without venal miseries and murderous hostilities. Positivistic man henceforth balanced societal transformation on superlatives of existence derived from a single and simple maxim—no religion, no warfare—a compelling attraction.

\/

---

25. Lindsell, *The New Paganism*, 62, "When [Voltaire] turned against religion in general and the Christian faith in particular, he became a never ending critic of the Catholic church."

26. Thatcher, *The Downing Street Years*, 11, "An internationalism which seeks to supersede the nation-state, however, will founder quickly upon the reality that very few people are prepared to make genuine sacrifices for it."

In the West VERTICALLY

With the philosophic spirits of Voltaire and Comte, Renaissance people, idealizing secularized human nature, tilted from the Enlightenment into even more positivistic nineteenth-century Modernism. Motivated by the spirit of autonomy, this distinctive dynamic maintained the Renaissance>Enlightenment>Modernism unity. What was once the exclusive territory of Roman Catholicism turned into rulership by individuals, each with the power of the self doing what was right in his/her own covetous eyes. Now humanism, more jealously secularizing, enlightened the West. In this philosophy, started in earliest Renaissance days, thinking circles copied the man seated on Peter's Chair in Rome; by negation of divinity, subsequent Enlightenment>Modernist legacies[27] placed numerous aristocratic individuals on thrones of power, mean gods and goddesses autocratically dominating the West. In this secularization human beings planned the future of the greatest vernacular civilization.[28]

Despite the Renaissance>Enlightenment>Modernism dominance, however, Roman Catholicism regained a life and Protestantism came into its own. The secularizers—now bitten by growing jealousy—organized political assistance to compel Westerners into the scientific world; restlessly intent on indisputable ascendancy, the humanist truth-makers demanded with singleness of purpose to own the West. For this purpose they fashioned and refashioned liberal governments to aid and abet secularization by legislative and educational measures. If the parents wanted Roman Catholicism and Protestantism, Modernists wanted the children. Liberal governments decided to enforce liberalism and compelled educational boards to indoctrinate students with humanist principles. Modernizing media at the same time pressed into homes and hearts the glories of humanism.[29]

---

27. Lindsell, *The New Paganism*, 48, "The old paganism of the Greeks and the Romans was now to become the source of inspiration for the new Enlightenment."

28. Saul, *The Unconscious Civilization*, 35, "The society in which legitimacy lives with the individual citizen is quite different. It can happily tolerate gods, kings and groups, providing they do not interfere with public good—that is, providing that they are properly regulated by the standards of the public good."

Dreher, *Live Not By Lies*, 53, "The Myth of Progress teaches that science and technology will empower individuals, unencumbered by limits imposed by religion and tradition, to realize their desires."

29. Packer and Howard, *Christianity*, 20, "Humanism set human beings at the center of the universe, maintaining that Nature, of which man is the most highly developed component, is all that exists; that happiness and enrichment of human life now is all that we should aim at; that scientific reason is the only tool needed for the task; and that religion hinders the enterprise rather than helps it."

SELF-EXAMINATION

Thus by its three pillars—governments, schools, and media—the Modernists inspired numerous Westerners to accept personal primacy in a manner that had escaped Roman Catholic popes, each Westerner more powerful in his/her own life than the men on Peter's Chair.

As the agricultural, industrial,[30] scientific, and technological revolutions pushed the West verging onto irrevocable change, the aristocracy benefits more people in the Bottom Tier.[31] Always adaptive in money-making, Modernist leaders through governments, schools, and multi-media dispersed throughout Bottom-Tier classes faith in science and advertised technological methodologies that persuaded all to live by the ultimate arbiters: the scientific truth, the scientific way, and the scientific life.[32] Consequently more Westerners, even within the religiosities, take in results of science and technology with pride and confidence. The religiosities too reinforce and secure humanist cultural values. By interweaving control into the very crevices and crannies of Bottom-Tier Western hearts, outspoken humanism wins.[33]

Through interiorizing Renaissance>Enlightenment>Modernist thinking, elitist decision-makers, unable to tolerate resistance for long, with the assistance of humanist mediators imposed social unity from one end of the West to the other by way of multiculturalism, one interpretation of which *unity in diversity*, another *divide and conquer*. Under the nascent assumption that this philosophical arrangement subdues opposition to humanism and must last forever, it secured, if not guaranteed, Protestant, Roman Catholic, and immigrant religiosities' submission to political

---

30. Ferguson, *Civilization*, 198, "That great economic transformation which historians long ago named the Industrial Revolution—that quantum leap in material standards of living for a rising share of humanity—had its origins in the manufacture of textiles."

31. Morgan, *Australia*, 18, "Few aristocrats emigrated to Australia as they had not needed to seek out opportunities in such a faraway destination. The social structure of colonial Australia was therefore heavily biased towards the bottom part of a vertical pyramid denoting social class."

32. Saul, *The Unconscious Civilization*, 9, " . . . the very size and prosperity of the elite permits it to interiorize an artificial vision of civilization as a whole. Thus, ours takes seriously only what comes from its own hundreds—indeed, thousands—of specialized sectors. Everything turns on internal reference." 34, "The human is thus reduced to a measurable value, like a machine or a piece of property. We can choose to achieve a high value and live comfortable or be dumped unceremoniously onto the heap of marginality."

33. Harari, *Homo Deus*, 259, "Whereas traditionally the great cosmic plan gave meaning to the life of humans, humanism reverses the roles and expects the experience of humans to give meaning to the universe."

manipulations; each entity within bad-tempered walls of multiculturalism abides by governments' hostility enforcing further spiritless existence.

At the same time Western religiosities, artificially divided, toiled with jealousy, lest one gain more aristocratic praise than another. To prevent that one gain precedence over another, all bow to the Modernist demand that nothing may be believed unless scientifically certified—according to repeatable evidence—and aristocratically approved. This educational method works on all levels[34] and for all ages, relegating questioners of the "truth" to agricultural back pastures; that is, enforced submission to shaming practices and re-schooling in the revolutionary fires of *Black Lives Matter*, *Antifa*,[35] and LGBTQ+/LGBTQQIP2AA radicals. From the Top Tier, strident aristocratic rulers bear down on the Bottom Tier to immerse coming generations into a meaningful whole by scientific sentience, from cradle to grave.[36]

\/

The shock at the violence of the First World War—the Great War, the war to end all wars—and the death of a generation of Western men unsettled Modernist confidence. Slowly, in opposition to Modernism, Postmodernism fostered another power play wherewith to entice the people of the West into its electro-magnetic heart. Overall, the two World Wars and then the United Nations' sinking ability at conflict management opened the abyss of relativism,[37] thus undermining the presupposed stability of modern self-assurance. This relativism turned and turns the self-interest of money-secure Top-Tier elite to promote Postmodernism, therewith to disrupt every critical engagement unfavorable to the aristocracy from the right as

---

34. Ferguson, *Civilization*, 51–52, "The West owes a debt to the medieval Muslim world, for both its custodianship of classical wisdom and its generation of new knowledge in cartography, medicine and philosophy as well as in mathematics and optics."

35. Hedges, *America*, 197, "The radical left and the radical right, each made up of people who have been cast aside by the cruelty of corporate capitalism, have embraced holy war. Their marginalized lives, battered by economic misery, have been filled with meaning. They hold themselves up as the vanguard of the oppressed. They claim the right to use force to silence those defined as the enemy."

36. Saul, *The Unconscious Civilization*, 24, "The aim of the ideologue is therefore to manipulate, trick or force the majority into acceptance."

37. Harpur, *God Help Us*, 39, "The average person might never even have heard of moral relativism, let alone be able to give an account of it or recognize that it is really the proper name for his or her outlook on conduct."

well as the left.[38] With insecurity everywhere at heart, Western aristocracy ably accelerates its autocracy.

Original proponents of this school of thought, men as Jacques Derrida, Jean-Francois Lyotard, and Michel Foucault,[39] spread the worth of relativism far, wide, and deep by questioning throughout the Bottom Tier the fundamentals of knowing and living.[40] This interrogative methodology deconstructing Western civilization imposed at the same time communist-inspired social constructs with which to shove the West over the edge into degradation, which unnerves Bottom-Tier residents into submitting to the Postmodern way, life, and truth, the three unquestionable pillars of liveliness in a nervous age.[41] In this dominance, Postmoderns oppose contradictory and contrarian Protestantism, Roman Catholicism, Jewish, and immigrant religiosities, fast-expanding Western entities. To own the West, relativists jostle and confuse Bottom-Tier fundamentals, thereby to enforce compliance with governmental, educational, and multi-media pressures by always questioning basic doctrines and ethics.

Relativism, as it immerses twenty-first century Westerners, dissolves the foundation of absolutes, demoralizing the certainties and the certitudes of right and wrong. Thus now the Modernist grip on the good and the evil slips away. Standards obvious and respected yet throughout the twentieth century now turn into relativistic ideals, actually Communist invented narcissistic moral and social devices once used to bewilder proletarian masses. Now these social constructs ridicule absolutes to repress Bottom-Tier

---

38. Saul, *The Unconscious Civilization*, 9, "The reaction of sophisticated elites, when confronted by their own failure to lead society, is invariably the same. They set about building a wall between themselves and reality by creating an artificial sense of well-being on the inside."

39. Smith, *Postmodernism*, 23.

These French Postmodernist philosophers found that Western society oppresses marginalized societies of the poor, non-white, or women through rich, white bourgeoisie males.

To be precise: Critical Race Theorists believe that Western institutions constitute systematically racist constrictions; traditional families, school systems, ecclesial structures, and political processes are white supremacist statements of oppression.

40. Proser, *Savage Messiah*, 155, "Postmodernism posits that reality is unknowable and meaningless. In attempting to overthrow traditional values, postmodernism dispenses with objective and transcendent truths that provide individuals with a realistic framework through which to perceive the world."

41. Proser, *Savage Messiah*, 156, "Postmodernists sort everyone into one of two groups: the oppressors and the victims; the latter of which suffer from systemic societal and cultural oppression at the hands of the former."

human beings from rebelling against Top-Tier social and political goals, at the same time activating indifference in the Bottom-Tier multitudes to the horrors of life. These social constructs proved the strength of communism:[42]

- The central fact of human existence is power and how it is used.
- There is no such thing as objective truth; there is only power.
- Identity politics sorts the oppressed from oppressors through a reductionist framework.[43]
- Intersectionality[44] is social justice ecumenism.
- Language creates human realities.

Left-wing authorities propagandize this way of communist social justice for the coming Western way of thinking and speaking. They change, and change, Western culture, making all submit to a despotism stronger than the now dispiriting Renaissance>Enlightenment>Modernism philosophical phenomena. The revelation of the beasts in Revelation 13 spells out its terrors.

Such Postmodern "rules" consist of unverifiable assurances, which make all reality conditional, somewhat akin to the 1930s Existentialism[45] in

---

42. Dreher, *Live Not By Lies*, 60–62.

43. Boyd, *Canadian Law*, 12. "Marxists have traditionally urged 'the withering away of the state' (and hence of law and legal order)." Thus they proposed the dictatorship of the proletariat.

44. Shapiro, *On the Right Side of History*, 199–200, intersectionality: " . . . human beings are members of various groups: racial groups, gender groups, religious groups, sexual orientation groups. And we can describe their 'lived realities' by referring to the intersection between those groups." 207, " . . . this new awareness of our intersectional problems will bring about a more *aware* world, and thus perhaps a better one."

45. More in Europe than in North America and Australasia, Existentialism restricted all burdened by insecurity to a view of man, who in concentrated ethical situations, had to make an instant decision based on feelings alive in the moment; each decision thus made meant the best course of action, understanding that situations constantly alter, either negating or affirming the worth of the decision. This philosophical movement emerged to counteract the Modernist organization-man.

Smith, *Postmodernism*, 18–19, " . . . a nebulous concept—a slippery beast eluding our understanding. Or perhaps better, postmodernism tends to be a chameleon taking on whatever characteristics we want it to: if it is seen as an enemy, postmodernism will be defined as monstrous; if it is seen as savior, postmodernism we be defined as redemptive." " . . . postmodernism, whether monster or savior, is something that has come slouching out of Paris. In particular, postmodernism owes its impetus to French philosophical influences." The whole is given to relativism.

SELF-EXAMINATION

which adepts made crucial decisions on the basis of active-in-the-moment feelings and temptations. In fact, ideologically possessed Postmoderns dissolve fundamentals and isolate Bottom-Tier society into pluralist/multicultural entities, each shot through with divide-and-conquer deviltry. Undone by multicultural segmentation—language barriers, religious commitments, and immigrant nationalities—*sociopathic*[46] Top-Tier elites pit Bottom-Tier hates against Bottom-Tier animosities, rendering with racial instability inoperative any civilization-wide one-family ideal. Given this multiculturalism, any consensus construction crumbles into regional gridlocks and private opinions.[47] Such pluralist preferences erode into endless regressions and drop down into dark places of covetousness. Stronger than regionalism, every person now comes with a private law system,[48] select rules of engagement, and instinctive urges with which to act out surges of greediness, provided no legal barrier or human right demands the contrary to such insatiability. Therefore, Top-Tier operatives induce anti-intellectualism with technological gadgetry to weaken coherences of stability and unity. In the chaos of the times greediness for money and the making of money further cordon off community building.

As Postmodernism assumes ownership of the West, forcing the rational meaningfulness of Modernism out of this civilization's core, the aristocracy hardens its inner motivation: more wants more. Confronting critical disruptions from other religiosities, aristocrats' power plays for wealth roughen. Meeting the resistance[49] Top-Tier denizens through street demonstrations, control over government legislation, and the structuring of educational programming will have the last word.

---

46. Hedges, *America*, 233.

47. Morgan, *Australia*, 27, "Multiculturalism needs to be more fully accepted and embedded through Australian society, however, before it can provide a firm basis for Australia's future destiny."
Steyn, *Lights Out*, 112, "If you want to appreciate the forces at play among western Muslims in societies hollowed out by multiculturalism, (Melanie Phillips') *Londonistan* is an indispensable read."

48. Boyd, *Canadian Law*, 5, "All of us will have opinions on these questions as well as justifications for our responses. For the law is a malleable human creation, which both reflects the movements of political actions and changing social mores, and influence those actors and more."

49. Ferguson, *Civilization*, 289, " . . . the West today is indeed awash with postmodern cults, none of which offers anything remotely as economically invigorating or socially cohesive as the old Protestant ethic."

In the West VERTICALLY

\/

While Postmodern relativizing eats away Modernism's certainties and certitudes, taking down also trinitarian, Christological, and ecclesiastical teachings, all Westerners struggle with the ungraspable crises of migratory movements, weather extremes, urban immensities, agricultural casualties, manufacturing revolutions, surface wreckages, and political disappointments, even as mammonism's embrace solidifies. In this clinching movement between physical perplexities and social disruptions an older generation may by flashbacks and reveries remember the firmness of Modernism even while sinking with Western civilization under the heavy weights of Postmodernism, now conforming to a different heart rhythm. Put cynically, over every horizon looms the emptiness invading the present. In these bewildering existential crises towering anxieties earmark fear of death[50] and skewer hope. For mortality is a given, even with immortality in mind. Unable to cover up the pains of uncertainty the wealthier seek cowering places under piles of cash.

\/

Out of the monetized heart of Western civilization personal, political, and commercial economies predict conversations and decisions. People talk of money, the default theme. Since money structures plans and inflates expectations, it enlivens multi-pronged dreams. By exchanging financial wisdom in major and minor communications, partners with undue reliance on and emboldened by scientific facts hope for the unstoppable progress of onrushing bull markets and earnings that exceed minimum wages by far.[51] In the dollar/euro suffused Top-Tier stratosphere, aristocrats choose and define economic interests, while everywhere else Western hearts overflow with money (non)sense.

In baring the Western heart, one powerful assumption holds forth. Beginning in the Top Tier, Westerners consider themselves money-wise

---

50. McKibben, *Falter*, 181, "We are, of course, the animal with consciousness, which is to say the animal that knows it will die. We don't dwell on it constantly, but it shapes us and the cultures we've constructed. The great psychologist Ernest Becker was convinced that Freud had it wrong: it wasn't sex that our minds repress, but the fear of death, and from that fear we've constructed everything from mighty pyramids to the mightier idea of heaven."

51. Greenspan, *The Age of Turbulence*, 269, "Regrettably, economic growth cannot produce lasting contentment or happiness."

people, people who know that without the necessary wherewithal life and happiness grind to a halt and fall apart. On the basis of money-sense Westerners in this post-Christian civilization consider themselves on the whole virtuous, each with a heart of gold, with an easily correctible fault here or there, nothing serious.[52] Comfortable with this self-evaluation, the evidence of self-righteousness builds up; before the gods and goddesses on the Top Tier Westerners are good people. Meanwhile aristocrats, determining the flow of human life throughout the West, set fast the monetized standard. This pacesetting of hearts yearns for the life that makes the West the West, demeans other civilizations, and earns merit with the aristocratic deities.

Top Tier Dread

Ever present fear of death with its extreme loss of wealth pokes and jabs Westerners in deepest personal complexities. Endless dark nothingness—night without sunrise—haunts reflective souls. In the implacable unease of death reliance on disposable incomes and bank accounts deflates, until even a penny is worthless for the purchase of immortality.

And death is near. From the Top Tier down, human life is cheap, if measured by mass shootings, addictions, suicides, homicides, femicides, and films with plots that glorify murder. Such statistics reveal the worth of each person, aristocrats equally.

In the Postmodern frame of reference, by devaluating Christianity, the fact that people make themselves or others into gods helps little against the forces of death: life on earth ends with the last sigh.[53] With awareness of dying insistent in the present, hauntings of death invade thoughts about money, money security now crumbling before the irreversibility of the loss of life. To the dismay even of Top-Tier residents, the humanistic rule of faith devastates also dollar/euro valuations hidden in off-shore tax havens and in the darkest corners of human hearts. As the meaninglessness

---

52. Harari, *Homo Deus*, 233, "... modernity is a surprisingly simple deal. The entire contract can be summarized in a single phrase: humans agree to give up meaning in exchange for power." The power of wealth.

53. Jones, *Darwin's Ghost*, xxvi, "Darwin's great idea—of life as a serious of successful mistakes—is simple, so simple, indeed, that it seems almost impossible that it could make such complicated things."

In the West Vertically

of money catches up,[54] dwellers at the top make final statements in the fires and flames of cremation; to the last breath they attempt to beat down the nullity that creeps into thoughtful moments before the door into death opens. Now the aristocrats' philosophy of meaning discovered in the Renaissance, empowered by the Enlightenment, and recast in the sciences of Modernism[55] struggles for grounding in and beyond Postmodernism.[56]

\/

For all the Top-Tier bravura at controlling the West, these gods and goddesses too vanish in the next Western version. In that other Western world the current deities will realize the insecurity in which they reign, for the coming pantheon will be brutally intolerant of old divinities, beasts cruelly tyrannous.

BOTTOM TIER DYNAMICS

Throughout the Bottom Tier rise and fall upper, middle, and lower classes, each category too poor for aristocracy. Here too life sucks. Each of these socio-economically regulated human communities fluctuates numerically. Some Bottom-Tier residents rise to the top. Some upper-class citizens sink to the bottom. Occasionally on account of sudden success in sports, films, and/or business a Westerner shoots up onto the Top Tier and social

---

54. Hedges, *America*, 45, "This nihilism, in its most radical form, is impervious to ethical critique and must be fought, as Nietzsche understood, with a matching religious fervor."

55. Marsden, *The Twilight of the American Enlightenment*, xxi, "Most mainstream mid-century American thinkers, who, like most modern thinkers, assumed collective intellectual progress, thought of themselves as having left such eighteenth-century enlightenment views behind. They were post-Darwinists who worked in a framework in which they took for granted human evolution and cultural evolution that shaped human beliefs and more."

56. Hedges, *America*, 248, "The platitudes about justice, equality, and democracy are just that. Only when ruling classes become worried about survival do they react. Appeal to the better nature of the powerful is useless. They don't have one."

Harari, *Homo Deus*, 84, in place of the Holocene, "Yet it may be better to call the last 70,000 years the Anthropocene epoch: the epoch of humanity. For during these millennia *Homo sapiens* became the single most important agent of change in global ecology."

Shapiro, *The Authoritarian Moment*, 88, "Postmodernism could be used to tear down any attempt to establish truth—even scientific facts could be rebutted by critiquing the way we define truth based on our cultural context."

acceptance among deified aristocrats. Beyond the financial rising and falling, the Bottom Tier's self-interested classes, each in its own way, long for saturation in the luxuries of lavish status symbols. These *securities* expressive of human hopes emulate aristocratic passions, only in much restricted ways. As Bottom-Tier populations also teeter and totter on the rim over which the disastrous, they bend to proletarian realities.

As bottom Bottom-Tier people drift about in variations and on different levels of despair, poverty, loss of identity, and crippling misery, others struggle with effervescent powers of dignity, purpose, pride, self-esteem, and sense of place that bewilder young and old; on the way down, lingering before the cusp of another West, classes and individuals according to the migratory order exchange more Western priorities for the weights of social constructs, thus sinking further into the heart of darkness.

Bottom Tier Militancy

By the end of the Second World War the West under American leadership celebrated an awesome victory over the Axis monstrosity, Nazi and Fascist,[57] both in the Atlantic and Pacific theaters. At the same time, across this hard-driving civilization generally, Westerners had had enough of fighting, wartime rationing, and travel restrictions. Post-1945 all with singular clarity longed for an era of peace.[58]

\/

Post-1945, obscenely appalling weapons of mass destruction kick-started a horrendous predicament for the Western psyche, at best a life under rising mushroom clouds.[59] The atomic bombs dropped on Hiroshima and Naga-

---

57. Bonhoeffer, Eberhard Bethge, tr., *Ethics*, 92, "Even the wars of the west have the unity of the west as their purpose."

Marsden, *The Twilight of the American Enlightenment*, xxv, "America had been thrust into world leadership, and this role accentuated the urgency of articulating ideals that would not only help bring unity out of diversity at home, but prove worthy of respect abroad."

58. Smith, *A Concise History of New Zealand*, 183, "Wartime controls only ended in 1950, allowing New Zealanders to look forward to an era of post-war growth and change . . . . In many respects they were, for the baby boomers (born from 1945 to 1961) who enjoyed a childhood unburdened by depression and war, and for the parents responsible for their upbringing."

59. Winchester, *Pacific*, 40, "The decision [President Harry] Truman made on that

saki transcended all experiences of international warfare. As possession of atomic and also more dreaded nuclear bombs volatilized potentials to end human history, Westerners understood that annihilation involved more than this civilization. When Russia also stockpiled these armaments and acquired necessary delivery systems the 1947–1991 Cold War engaged the West and the world with existential tensions.[60] In that troubled age hundreds of millions at first trembled and slept fitfully, dreaming about safety in public bomb shelters and private bunkers. At the onset of the Cold War, the fact of global annihilation,[61] nervously considered, sank deep into Western consciousness and fear of warring suffused the West: *not this kind of bloody chaos, ever!* Facing the unthinkable made foresighted détente acceptable,[62] even as an unfamiliar and seemingly shaky truce troubled and diminished the post-War triumph of Western liberal democracy.

Full-scale nuclear obliteration and resultant winter conditions seem now inconceivable, given treaties of non-aggression and destruction of nuclear stockpiles.[63] Still, remnant Russian and America accruals, along

---

third Thursday of January, as well as his formal order to the Atomic Energy Commission that followed, was to start a program of work on a very different kind of device, and a type both of unimaginable deadliness and theoretically limitless destructive power."

Possession of fusion bombs and thermonuclear devices edged the West into a horrific tomorrow. At the first thermonuclear test, 70, "The iron gates guarding some terrible inferno seemed to clang wide open and unleash a ball of fire and shock waves and roarings of unimaginable speed, violence, and loudness. A white fireball four miles across was created in less than one second."

60. Smith, *A Concise History of New Zealand*, 185, "After 1945 the external threat of the Cold War shaped defence policy. Indeed the fear of communism drove New Zealand into the Cold War—much like the fear of racial degeneracy inspired defence strategy before it—alongside Australia as a small partner in the Western alliance led by the United States against countries led by the Soviet Union."

Morgan, *Australia*, 98, "The end of the Cold war in 1989 seemed to herald the beginning of a new era of international peace in which the threat of the spread of Communism was diminished and former Communist countries reintegrated into Western notions of democracy."

61. Harari, *Homo Deus*, 309, "Liberal democracy was saved only by nuclear weapons. NATO adopted the MAD doctrine (Mutual Assured Destruction), according to which even conventional Soviet attacks would be answered by an all-out nuclear strike."

62. Schell, *The Fate of the Earth*, 21, "But since we cannot afford under any circumstances to let a holocaust occur, we are forced in this one case to become the historians of the future—to chronicle and commit to memory an event that we have never experienced and must never experience.'

63. Harpur, *God Help Us*, 16, 'Apart from ongoing, grave concerns over who exactly controls the nuclear weapons in the Soviet arsenal, it remains true that both the United

SELF-EXAMINATION

with the Israeli, Iranian, Indian, and North Korean accumulations of nuclear weaponry, enforce living under the gloom of mutual deterrence, nothing ever secure, in which climate more germination and aggression of Postmodern relativizing. This life is ever moving onto the unstable verge, verging, of peace or war.

Not that the West eschews fighting—far from home and in others' backyards. The inconclusive histories of war on the Korean Peninsula,[64] the 1962 Cuban missile crisis, in Vietnam,[65] over Iraq, over the Falkland Islands (1982),[66] IRA terrorism (1979–1990), Gulf Wars, al-Qaida,[67] against the Afghan Taliban, currently over Iran's nuclear technology,[68] and countering cyber-attacks every which way prove the point while registering these as failures of UN policing. Now in the shadows of the above unsettled military adventures, under NATO and UN umbrellas Western troops as peace-makers rather than as traditional peace-keepers restrain Chinese as well as Russian dreams, their bellicosity notwithstanding.[69] The effective-

---

States and its Soviet counterparts still possess many thousands of deadly ballistic missiles capable of wiping out civilization as we know it several times over."

64. Winchester, *Pacific*, 152, "No peace treaty has ever been enacted between the various sides in that brutal three-year brawl: the 1953 agreement merely established rules meant to prevent the resumption of armed hostilities. Considering that today the principal parties have atomic weapons, these rules seem more necessary than ever."

65. Winchester, *Pacific*, 206, "The Vietnamese path to independence, of shedding their submission to a European power, was long and bloody."

66. Thatcher, *The Downing Street Years*, 173, "We were defending our honour as a nation, and principles of fundamental importance to the whole world—above all, that aggressors should never succeed and that international law should prevail over the use of force."

67. Rogan, *The Arabs*, 483, on September 11, 2001 Arabian terrorists attacked the World Trade Center, the heart of Western economic forces. "We can only surmise from subsequent statements by al-Qaida the kinds of changes the suicide hijackers had in mind: to drive America from the Muslim world, to destabilize pro-Western regimes in the Muslim world, to overturn those regimes and replace them with Islamic states." This attack intensified throughout Arabian worlds other terrorist wars against the West.

68. Abrahamian, *A History of Modern Iran*, 195, "The USA-Iran rivalry has recently focused on the highly explosive issue of nuclear technology. Iran vehemently insists on the right to develop such technology, citing international law, the need to find energy alternatives, and the inalienable right of developing countries to enter the modern world by harnessing what it sees to be the cutting edge of science."

69. Winchester, *Pacific*, 28, "The Pacific Ocean—now almost freed from its former European control, yet brimming with new disputes, a region that is tectonically and meteorologically dangerous—is ringed with nations undergoing immense internal change, is unimaginably busy with commerce, and has come to be at the forefront of science and

ness of restraining Western belligerence, even as a final recourse, depends actually on the aristocracy's aggressive demands for making money. Meanwhile, this world drifts into catastrophes beyond compare.

Bottom Tier Corporatism[70]

The economic ideology, corporatism, originated in the nineteenth century, a reinvention of feudal guilds,[71] wherewith to control the flow of finances, own the loyalty of Bottom-Tier peoples, and more sinisterly, undermine democracy. Managing individualism and individual voters through workers unions, industrial conglomerations, professional associations, and governmental licensing bureaucracies give the elite through the authority of riches the ability to direct Western citizens in the purchase of goods and services as well as voting patterns that enrich Top-Tier aristocrats. Corporatism thus forges Western society into *addicts*, people who depend for life, food, and space on socially and morally liberal covetousness. This dependency allows the aristocracy to persuade Bottom-Tier voters for which political party to cast ballots, in this process undermining the legitimacy of democratic freedom. Rather than search out the common good, Bottom-Tier voters now seek advancement in self-interest, each as covetous as the members of the aristocracy.[72]

Corporatism is an ideology by which unions, conglomerates, and associations claim rational self-interest in decision-making, not the good entitlements of democracy.[73] This ideology reduces Bottom-Tier Westerners

---

self-discovery."

70. Frankly, I am indebted to Saul's *The Unconscious Civilization* for insights into corporatism.
Thatcher, *The Downing Street Years*, 751, "[In Germany] it had become a kind of corporatist, highly collectivized, 'consensus'–based economic system, which pushed up costs, suffered increasingly from market rigidities and relied on qualities of teutonic self-discipline to work at all."

71. Boyd, *Canadian Law*, 20, feudalism: " . . . the political and economic system that granted nobility and land in exchange for the labour and military service of serfs and vassals on the land."

72. Saul, *The Unconscious Civilization*, 3, "The point of these received wisdoms of the second half of the twentieth century is that the very heart and soul of our 2,500-year-old civilization is, apparently, economics, and from that heart flowed, and continues to flow, everything else." Economics! Money!

73. Shapiro, *The Authoritarian Moment*, 37, "Corporations, petrified of legal liability—or at least hoping to avoid accusations of insensitivity or bigotry—have caved to

to passive and conforming citizens who only hurt themselves if they object to the goods, services, and policies offered.⁷⁴ This changes Westerners from a people upholding democracy into men and women who deny the liberties of speech and movement, and at times absorb unbearable levels of unemployment, debt, inflation, and restrictions in national economies. Refuse union membership? Reject pensions? Hunt without permits? Raise a large family of socially productive children? Walk away from unemployment insurance? Decline licensing? Circumvent formal education? Contradict euthanasia? Oppose abortion? Deny trending LBGTQ+ orientation? Communicate outside social mediate platforms? Through denial of democratic reality the West sinks into its corporate monolatry, money.

Bottom Tier History

With the aristocrats, Western civilization's Bottom-Tier inhabitants toil at the top of the evolutionary chain,⁷⁵ to survive as well as dominate over pandemics, insects, and wild life. This history of evolution, unchecked by divine fiat, stretches out of the original cosmic night through incomprehensible aeons onto the edge of hungry morrows. This evolutionistic hope? A future livelier than the deadly past. ⁷⁶

According to the reigning scientific hypothesis the history that shaped and still shapes Western civilization oozed out of boiling oceans and fetid morasses, then over multi-millennial eras slogged through

---

[woke] culture. They have enforced a culture of silence in which tens of millions of employees fear speaking their minds for fear of retaliation."

74. Saul, *The Unconscious Civilization*, 19, "The history of [the twentieth century]—demonstrated in part by its unprecedented violence—suggests that our addiction is getting worse. We have already swept through the religions of world empires based upon the intrinsic superiority of each nation or race of empire builders, on through Marxism and Fascism, and now we are enthralled by a new all-powerful clockmaker god—the marketplace—and his archangel, technology."

Gillam, *Whitewash*, 113, "Many . . . corporate powers, including those in the agrochemical industry, have long histories of defending themselves against claims that they covered up the dangers of injury from asbestos, polychlorinated biphenyls (PCBs), Agent Orange, or other chemicals."

75. Harari, *Homo Deus*, 85, "During all [the] aeons, whether you were a virus or a dinosaur, you evolved according to the unchanging principles of natural selection."

76. Du Bois, *The Soul of Black Folks*, 114, "War, murder, slavery, extermination, and debauchery,—this has again and again been the result of carrying civilization and the blessed gospel to the isles of the sea and the heathen without the law."

indescribable perils. And, portentously, in the midst of the present millennium, approximately 600,000 years ago, restless *homo sapiens* walked out an African past over the Eastern Mediterranean land bridge into a Northern European future. In the takeover the original Westerners pushed Neanderthal populations over the tipping point and carved out an outsized base for living amidst towering forests and omnivorous predators. In this evolutionary process, by happenstance, Westerners as Modernists arrived in the nineteenth and twentieth centuries of the Common Era in search of sunlit horizons.

\/

Modernists, by the nineteenth century, dominated the Western convergence of people; they sought generation upon generation, ceaselessly, to transcend the past in the evolutionary manner for a future that extends beyond the Moon, beyond Mars even, eventually to originate a new humankind culturally progressive and bionically reinforced to cheat death, sentient beings peacefully at home in the great galactic unknown with more complex life-forms. This next civilization, sanitized of religiosities, stuffed with virtues, and hence freed from barbaric ferocities may now light up Western hopes. Liberated from sectarian rivalry and competitive madness, humankind then moves to where no one has gone before by creating an outright new race. Preparations for meeting superior sentient races makes the earth seem more than a tiny orb glowing weakly in a cold and lonely void.

The West, radically reconstructed by Renaissance hopefulness for a thoroughly rational humanity, came alive in a scientifically ordered civilizational structure. Now Westerners design governments, schools, businesses, families, and citizens in conformity with intellectually precise human planning. In this world free from divine interdictions and thunderings of angry gods, Westerners junked the traditional markers of the Roman Catholic's Middle Ages and scrapped the metaphysical pointers of Protestant religiosity, finally to work out a rigorous Aristotelianism.[77] This resurging of Aristotelian-structured rationalism mobilized the Western mind; with the power of philosophical, mechanical, industrial, and technological thinkers, national governments now recognized, studied, and regulated the historical process in order to arrive at an earthly heaven or a heavenly earth, as they

---

77. Mohammedans collected, translated, interpreted ancient Greek philosophy, Aristotelianism included, and carried the whole into Western universities.

do to this day. More precisely, aristocrats in the development of Western culture[78] cater to the urbanity of Bottom-Tier happiness, a happiness dead to revolutionary agitation.

John Locke, 1632-1704, Adam Smith, 1723-1790, and David Hume,[79] 1711-1776 for money-making and Auguste Comte with mind-making interjected into the Occident a civilizational goal with which to point out its humanistic destination. In its way the Renaissance followed by the Enlightenment broke free from every divinely appointed destiny for the commonality of purely rational living.[80] After the Renaissance the more secularizing Enlightenment and the even stronger rationalizing Modernism fought (positivism =) historicism[81] with its deterministic negatives that displaced and rejected Western humanism.

Historicism allowed more humanistic control over governments and nations to reinvent the Western destiny. As long as Westerners in civilizational development considered the West the epicentric motor force of world history, every assessment of the future anticipated progressive ideals

---

78. Smith, *Postmodernism*, 21, "We take culture seriously by taking ideas seriously."

Harari, *Homo Deus*, 235-236, "Modern culture is the most powerful in history, discovering and growing. At the same time, it is plagued by more existential angst than any previous culture."

79. Lindsell, *The New Paganism*, 71, "He argued that the facts of reality are only made certain by probability. If this is true there can be no metaphysics and neither the existence of God nor the existence of the physical world can be demonstrated by reason."

80. Marsden, *The Twilight of the American Enlightenment*, xxii, "[Mid-century thinkers] also shared with eighteenth-century leaders a confidence that rational and scientific understandings were essentially objective and therefore should be normative."

81. Dooyeweerd, *In the Twilight of Western Thought*, 62, "Radical historicism makes the historical viewpoint the all-encompassing one, absorbing all the other aspects of the human experiential horizon. Even the religious center of human experience . . . is reduced to a flowing stream of historical moments of consciousness. All our scientific, philosophical, ethical, aesthetic, political and religious standards and conceptions are views as the expression of the mind of a particular culture or civilization." Historicism closely resembles positivism.

Oreskes and Conway, *The Collapse of Western Civilization*, 36, "This [positivism or historicism or Baconianism] held that through experience, observation, and experiment, one could gather reliable knowledge about the natural world, and that this knowledge would empower its holder."

Boyd, *Canadian Law*, 7, "Positivism is rooted in the British doctrine of parliamentary supremacy. This doctrine . . . dictates that Parliament is supreme: Parliament can make or unmake any law, and no person or body shall override or set aside its legislation."

Dreher, *Live Not By Lies*, 52, " . . . a philosophy built on the idea that science was the source of all authoritative knowledge."

IN THE WEST VERTICALLY

on sunlit horizons. Believing this radical cultivation of life—designed partially for overloading the Bottom Tier with contentment—drives through financial policies, corporate decisions, industrial productivity, and above all advanced academics to the ultimate state. This engaging vision, a civilization rooted in the Renaissance's heaven-on-earth perspective, carries forward an ideal from the Middle Ages. This internalized visioning energizes Westerners with moral superiority.

Before moving on, an aside: Westerners due to travel and trade recognized other civilizations' existence.[82] In this geographical awakening to the larger world,[83] the effects of pride multiplied in the conviction that stagnant Arabian, African, and Oriental civilizations were incapable of thorough modification and modernization. The West thus assumed its king-of-the-mountain stance.

\/

In the early twentieth century philosophers as Oswald Spengler[84] and historians as Arnold Toynbee[85] deflected the positivity of Modernism;

---

82. Dooyeweerd, *In the Twilight of Western Thought*, explaining historicism, 62, "Each civilization has arisen and ripened in the all-embracing stream of historical development."

Ferguson, *Civilization*, 20, "As late as 1776 Adam Smith could still refer to China as 'one of the richest, that is, one of the most fertile, best cultivated, most industrious, and most populous countries in the world . . . a much richer country than any part of Europe."

83. Actually, the awakening to other civilizations began in the AD 1680–1715 decades: Hazard, *The European Mind*, 11, "Perspectives changed. Concepts which had occupied the lofty sphere of the transcendental were brought down to the level of things governed by circumstance. Practices deemed to be based on reason were found to be mere matters of custom, and, inversely, certain habits which, at a distance, had appeared preposterous and absurd, took on an apparently logical aspect once they were examined in the light of their origin and local circumstances."

84. Toynbee, *Civilization On Trial*, 9, " . . . Oswald Spengler's *Untergang des Abendlandes*. As I read those pages teeming with firefly flashes of historical insight, I wondered at first whether my whole inquiry had been disposed of by Spengler before even the questions, not to speak of the answers, had fully taken shape in my own mind." 10, " . . . when I looked in Spengler's book for an answer to my question about the geneses of civilization, I saw that there was still much for me to do, for on this point Spengler was, it seemed to me, most unilluminatingly dogmatic and deterministic. According to him, civilizations arose, developed, declined, and foundered in unvarying conformity with a fixed time-table, and no explanation was offered for any of this. It was just a law of nature, which Spengler had detected, and you must take it on trust from the master: *ipse dixit*."

85. Ferguson, *Civilization*, 258, "When you reflect on what caused the fall of ancient

they found the Renaissance's idealized future fictitious and its scientific humanity unpredictable, if not inconceivable. These pessimists, from within the confines of historicism, excised from history every sort of hope for a meaningful civilization governing all reality. Injecting negativity and deconstruction into tomorrow's philosophical and historical adventures, they thereby publicized the foreboding consequences of historicism. Proponents of historicism thus modified the liveliness of culture[86] and reduced the human intellect with its daily rounds of activity to meaningless influences on the future of the West, convinced that civilizations live and die by deterministic forces.

As historicism negatively hemmed in Modernist ideals, believing the Renaissance's entrenched belief in human reasoning rippled away on Postmodernist relativities, its widening circles falling flat. Western superiority through scientific modes of thoughts and dominated by industrial/technological productivity no longer favored this civilization, its fate changing, and changing.

\/

In the decline of Modernist exaggeration and the rise of historicist darkness, darkness dominated by Postmodernism, a dominating feature of humanity came out of deep time: humankind's irrepressible and irresistible religious heart. However much Voltaire and Comte's followers scoffed at religiosity in its three-phase theology>metaphysics>science predictability, nevertheless commanding religiosities and authoritative values ate away at now cold and tired Modernism with its dark and fateful historicism, Postmodernism increasing the gloom.

Rome, such fears (of a civilizational collapse) appear not altogether fanciful. Economic crisis; epidemics that ravaged the population; immigrants overrunning the imperial borders; the rise of a rival empire—Persia's—in the East; terror in the form of Alaric's Goths and Attila's Huns."

86. Dooyeweerd, *In the Twilight of Western Thought*, 91, "The cultural mode of formation reveals itself in two directions. On the one hand it is a formative power over persons unfolding itself by giving cultural form to their social existence; on the other, it appears as a controlling manner of shaping natural materials."

Marsden, *The Twilight of the American Enlightenment*, 7, " . . . in a capitalistic society, mass culture inevitably had a parasitic relationship with high culture."

Hedges, *America*, 17, "If we do not know our history and our culture, if we accept the history and the culture manufactured for us by the elites, we will never free ourselves from the forces of oppression."

In the West Vertically

In the Postmodern gloom radical religious energies, communism with its liberty-impairing evils not the least,[87] shift the West farther onto the edge, slowly down-bound into other dire calamities. Because of World Wars, thermo-nuclear fears, and bloody insurrections in Third World countries the ultimate hope of humanism imploded with astonishing, indeed, frightening clarity.[88] As post-1945 chaotic Modernism's relativizing tumbled about positivism/historicism, multiculturalist visionaries still promised a *sinless* world, a global civilizations emanating out of the West. For this human commonality the powers-that-be blueprinted an all-absorbing drive to restrict religiosity behind barriers, ban racism, forbid slander, legalize immoralities, and tolerate perversities thus to formulate the idyllic life. In that cultural arena, the religiosities balled together under political oversight working together, each entity—Protestant, Roman Catholic, and the numerous immigrant communions as Hindus, Buddhists, Mohammedans, and others—must co-exist within physical limitations, each free and happy in its fenced-off sphere.[89]

Moreover, once repressed minorities and marginalized immigrant groups now find copious oxygen in Postmodernism. In the power of multiculturalism they demand financial restitution for lived experiences of discrimination and with the vocal resonance of law-suits insist on indemnity. Secondly, they find notoriety in the courts of public opinion by toppling statues and in name-changes.[90] Thirdly, they claim political recognition. With impacts on governments, educational institutions, and name changes, these anti-Aryan minorities will have Caucasians make space for co-governing the West by denying essentially traditional—*white*—title to lands within national boundaries and find strength in sufficient numbers to claim co-ownership, at the least. Each "victory" in the courts and claims

---

87. Ferguson, *Civilization*, 207, "The essence of Marxism was the belief that the industrial economy was doomed to produce an intolerably unequal society divided between the bourgeoisie, the owners of capital, and the propertyless proletariat."

88. Ferguson, *Civilization*, 175, 'As the twentieth century dawned, Germany was in the vanguard of Western civilization."

89. Steyn, *Lights Out*, 114, "... nations die—not by war or conquest, but by a thousand trivial concessions, until one day you wake up and you don't need to sign a formal instrument of surrender because you did it piecemeal."

90. Smith, *A Concise History of New Zealand*, 9, "Naming is a political act."
Fukuyama, *Identity*, 7, "A humiliated group seeking restitution of its dignity carries far more emotional weight than people simply pursuing their economic advantage."

of ownership by squatters' rights builds a bridging system to consume the whole of the West.[91]

Now belief in and recognition of this other, Postmodern, vision also motivates front-running Westerners to relativize the hardness of national boundaries; at the same time they acknowledge Asian, African, West Indian, Russian, as well as south American entities as more than competing civilizations. Through money-speak they participate in corporate, pan-national partnerships. In this widening globalization the West means less, international markets more. As the ideal of scientific humanity wears off, economic solidarity raises more monetary covetousness.

Even as the hungry hands of multiculturalism close in and national boundaries shrink in significance, utopian multiculturalists compile another Western meta-narrative.[92] Meanwhile, designed with aristocratic complicity, dreamful multiculturalists envision for this new world the absence of venality, release from misery however defined, as well as freedom from military hostilities. This pretentious multicultural harmonizing with wokeist aggression seems to present the best of all worlds, socialist/communist style, to produced aristocratic wealth. The advance into soft tyranny secures ugly wokeist intolerance and deadens ideals for a reinvented West.

\/

Currently, Western civilization confronts transitioning-into-worse totalitarian regimes; Russian, Chinese, North Korean, and Iranian come to mind, the Indian less so. Those beguiling standard bearers of aggression

---

91. Lindsell, *The New Paganism*, 143, "The laws of a nation are a mirror that reflects the world and life view of the people of that nation. When the world and life view changes, the laws that are in accord with the displaced world and life view change too over a period of time long or short."

92. Steyn, *Lights Out*, 10, "Multicultural societies are so invested in 'tolerance' that they'll tolerate the explicitly intolerant (and avowedly unicultural) before they'll tolerate anyone pointing out that intolerance."

Packer and Howard, *Christianity*, 22, "Inside its velvet glove of tolerance is an iron hand of tyranny; its professed compassion becomes a sanction for cruelty, and its professed humanitarianism a kind of inhumanity."

Shapiro, *The Authoritarian Moment*, 49, "John Dewey, perhaps the most influential early progressive, believed ... that the state could act as the moving force behind utopian ambition."

Harpur, *God Help Us*, 39, "As societies become ever more pluralistic, and as the traditional influence of established religions continues to decline, relativism means that there is a decreasing ability to find a moral consensus on anything."

with nuclear arms and multitudinous troops, men as well as women, indoctrinated to antagonize the West will fight with pent-up absurdities of obedience. Tyrants at the top stoop to destroy the world and themselves, if only thereby to grind Western civilization into more of the dust of history. Rather than seek peace and prosperity for all possible within a cohesive global community, despots see fertile expedients in tyranny.

As the stability of the West since the Second World War falters, American leadership economically and militarily still imposes its will, mortifying rogue military ambitions; the protective American umbrella over law-and-order governments asserts an essential decency, an absence of international strife in the West. Because of the United States' prominence in upholding Western civilization against dictatorial aggression, Top-Tier aristocrats benefit first from American imperialism arranging and rearranging the affairs of the nations.

Fears of nuclear conflagration and scorching death reinforce America's protective arm; these fears also unite Western peoples. As perverse dictatorial rulers scheme to afflict Western nations with vassalage or colonial status, pressures to unify in military defense and economic strength intensify. With global invectives of hatred based less on rational judgment and more on perverse tribal delusions, despots without twinges of sympathy psychopathically visualize the worth of military aggression.

Ever sensitive, Westerners through governments acting in cohesive fraternities as NATO and ANZUS and the singularly appealing democratic ideals relevant throughout the prolonged Cold War once again rise up, necessary for more than mere existence; for univocal unity in the face of unscrupulous hatred,[93] the West needs fight for its democratic liberties and unalienable rights. Freedom against looming international madness of soul stands out as an invaluable beacon of light, except to left-wing and right-wing minorities agitating with Western largesse against Western democracy. Westerners, as the greatest force for political liberty that the world has known, aptly honor democratic hopes, even as aristocratic tyrants push this civilization over to the brink into other environments wherein to reevaluate political currents as well as personal commitments to democracy.[94]

---

93. Ferguson, *Civilization*, 236, "If the Cold War had ever become hot, the Soviet Union would very likely have won it. With a political system far better able to absorb heavy losses . . . the Soviet Union also had an economic system that was ideally suited to the mass production of sophisticated weaponry."

94. Saul, *The Unconscious Civilization*, 34, " . . . we live in a corporatist society with soft pretensions to democracy. More power is slipping every day towards the groups." 36,

Self-Examination

As negations of Western truths, impositions of social constructs, and combinations of ego-centric minorities weaken this civilization's heartlands, the elites, gods and goddesses all, dispute its frontiers and dismiss its democratic resolves. The wonderful inventions of the past and the technological wizardry of the present that improve living standards and raise the envy of neighboring civilizations now serve internally operating Postmodern interests, multicultural minorities, Chinese colonizing,[95] and aristocratic covetousness. Unable to generate creatively new vistas of hope, in-house adversaries prefer activism on the depressive brink of unresolved diversities to incite more hatreds with which to consume this civilization.[96]

\/

Over the West, as over larger worlds, hover five concurrently sobering and unmoving clouds. One: fear of the numerous ballistic missiles poised for asymmetric warfare balanced by weak détentes. Two: ecological desolation mired in devastations of drought and flood, storms and heatwaves, polluted waters and desert sands, pandemics and addictions balanced by unpredictable governmental perceptions of crisis. Three: massing multicultural hatreds balanced by anti-racist appeals. Unresolved, these three lead first the West into unfathomable and ungovernable anxieties that repudiate global conciliation.[97] Four: Sino-invasions balanced by sleeping governments. And five: covetous aristocratic leadership balanced by providential hubris. Under these sinister cloud formations change dominates the West's historical narrative. On the cusp of its gradual exit many disturbing tomorrows identify the Occident's dropping away past the tipping-point into dark savagery.

"Clearly the democratic mechanisms are still in place and the citizens do occasionally succeed in imposing a direction upon the elites."

95. Manthorpe, *Claws of the Panda*, 13, "Canada has become a battleground on which the Chinese Communist Party seeks to terrorize, humiliate, and neuter its opponents."

96. McKibben, *Falter*, 1, "Put simply, between ecological destruction and technological hubris, the human experiment is now in question."

97. Harari, *Homo Deus*, 19, " . . . cyber warfare may destabilise the world by giving even small countries and non-state actors the ability to fight superpowers effectively."

Bottom Tier Education

Out of mightily expanding reverberations of the Renaissance, its leaders' rational counsel insisted on quality education, steadying indoctrination in humanist values. Throughout Western civilization the aristocratically controlled and popularly elected governments instituted the public school system.[98] In time, governments through departments of education mandated, informed, and financed schooling, for young girls as well. In a steadily broadening educational system, students absorbed more than basic skills in reading, writing, and arithmetic. As leaders of national public school systems with the aid of teachers pushed Protestant and Roman Catholic convictions aside, they intended schooling to serve for the greater good of the humanist tradition, confirming the earliest Renaissance intentions. This humanist tradition worked as the powerful key to the continuation of democracy. As children learned to appreciate the intentions and institutions of democracy as the road to prosperity, they reflected on democratic fundamentals, uploading in the process the way of the West.[99]

\/

Since the Second World War, evasions of the Protestant and Roman Catholic convictions along with slippages in the quality of public education troubled growing contingents of parents. One evidence of this concerning appeared in the building of private, parentally governed school systems, each in every Western country opposed to the public schools. As the children of apprehensive fathers and mothers walked out of public school systems, taking Protestant and Roman Catholic convictions as well as ethics with them, and entered into parentally controlled elementary/secondary institutions, government funded educators in departments of education perceived an opening into the minds of students to teach large majorities the relativizing new mathematics, social studies instead of Western history, and standardizing vernacular languages.[100] This indoctrination of students with multicultural mores persuaded other parents to extend the exodus out

---

98. In England, public schools served elite elements in society.
Ferguson, *The Great Degeneration*, 125, " . . . in my opinion, the best institutions in the British Isles today are the independent schools."

99. Lindsell, *The New Paganism*, 42, "It may be said that as the schools go, so goes the nation." Or the civilization.

100. Shapiro, *On the Right Side of History*, 40, "The promulgators of multiculturalism in education all too often aren't promoting breadth of learning, but lack of learning."

of the public school structures. These fathers and mothers willingly pay government public school taxes and, at the same time, bear the expenditures for private schooling, out of the conviction that sons and daughters in non-governmental-controlled schools receive a better than average education. The numerically increasing private schools expose on the educational landscape an uneasy mutating in Western values, parents seeking release for children from revolutionizing forms of education.

A second decline in public school systems across the West enters with immigrant demands. Muslims want offspring educated in the Mohammedan way. Hindus seek indoctrination of children in the Hindu tradition. Buddhists spreading everywhere through Western societies infiltrate educational processes with Buddhist practices. In elementary and secondary systems teachers instill equal respect for all in the multicultural manner, always at the expense of the Renaissance ideals, one of which the elimination of religiosities. Permeation of foreign (religious!) educational values relativizes everything. In colleges and universities Muslim, Hindu, and Buddhist instructors, to name these only, promote agendas in contrast to the Renaissance>Enlightenment>Modernist vision; they introduce foreign mentalities to which weak governments concede.[101] Whatever anti-racist hopes may cleave to this incorporation of anti-Western immigrants into the publicly funded educational systems, each concession contributes to the decline of public education, the erosion of democratic ideals, and the breakup of Western unity.[102] These overall school agendas lead the people of this civilization onto and into many changes and disturbances now still strange to the imagination.

---

101. Shapiro, *The Authoritarian Moment*, 37, "Universities, once bastions of free thought, are now philosophical one-party systems dedicated to the promulgation of authoritarian leftism."

102. Proser, *Savage Messiah*, 211, "One of the base notes in the death knell of Western universities was the shutting down of free speech, and with it, exposure to diverse viewpoints, the essential value of a traditional university education." 218, "... university students [who] were not exposed to intellectually diverse viewpoints and so those who lacked strong opinions, or personalities, were being intellectually overwhelmed by the predominantly progressive atmosphere created by instructors, administrators, and fellow students."

Shapiro, *The Authoritarian Moment*, 34, quoting one Roger Scruton, "In place of the old beliefs of a civilization based on godliness, judgment and historical loyalty, young people are given the new beliefs of a society based on equality and inclusion, and are told that the judgment of other lifestyles is a crime." Except the condemnation of Western culture and lifestyle.

A third.[103] As multicultural interests—aboriginal, communist, socialist, and racist—break racialist tethers and insist upon decolonizing educational systems, they claim recognition in the schools for traditional beliefs and/or political ideals, through qualified teachers. Through Western largesse and educational systems they will have nothing less than the indoctrination of children in the aboriginal, communist, socialist, and racist fundamentals. Again, multicultural-conscious governments submit to the erosion of the West in the name of and to the detriment of democratic standards, allowing oppositional traditions to bastardize the essentials of democracy, because newcome immigrant communities will have growing room for alien provocations.

One more humiliation of public education—more pronounced since 1945—comes from corporate domineering by pouring more funds into higher education. Tech moguls and industrial magnates, deities of the West, seek students with managerial potential, to train these men and women to uphold the aristocratic influence over the Bottom Tier.[104] This shift in postsecondary education destabilizes more the original public commitment for acquiring and promoting democratic values.

\/

The less students in elementary and secondary schools learn to think about and reflect on what they hear, see, and read, each lacks the basic Western academic tools with which to personalize the good of the West and reject

---

103. Shapiro, *On the Right Side of History*, 40, "Western civilization, in the view of many on the radical Left, was a bastion of imperialism and racism; students should be devoted to learning about those shortcomings, rather than about the glories of ancient philosophy." 41, "This is a dramatic, deliberate misreading of the history of Western civilization—the greatest force for good in world history."

104. Saul, *The Unconscious Civilization*, 69, "The central theme today revolves around 'quality,' which actually means that the emphasis should go onto feeding the best up through the system to the elite structures. This is the standard hierarchical, corporatist approach." In other words, 70, "The universities have become to a great extent the handmaidens of the corporate system."

Packer and Howard, *Christianity*, 21, "Humanist leaders prove again and again to be profound pessimists, aristocratically contemptuous of human nature as it is and optimistic only about their plans for changing it."

Lindsell, *The New Paganism*, 135, "Colleges and universities have not only imbibed deeply from the well of the new Weltanschauung, they have also been prominent in the spread of paganism."

alien influences.[105] Thus they become pliable tools of the aristocrats and with them head over the edge into for now grimy shadows. Thoughtless victims of advertising schemes, governmental policies, and societal shifts, Bottom-Tier residents ignorantly follow first the worst of ego-centric leaders.

Bottom Tier Family

Since 1945, marriages and families break up in ways and to degrees unknown for generations.[106] By imitation of the Western pantheon, a collective as hopelessly immoral as once fornicative Greek deities on Mount Olympia, Bottom-Tier residents fragment the basic building blocks of society. On account of divorce, absentee fathers,[107] poverty, alcoholism, opioid addiction, individualism, adultery, homosexualism, pederasty, multi-media preoccupations, and other selfish factors, the people of the Bottom Tier descent together onto the edge of the unknown. Once considered crucial to the solidarity of Western society, Westerners now fracture and destabilize society by degrading marriage/family bonds perilously, damages to children most reprehensible. Now, by way of *private initiatives* at immorality they of the West contribute to this age of disorder, toleration beyond limits.[108] Western open-mindedness permits every ethical mutability. With exceptions, Westerners, in abject emulation of the gods and goddesses, limit families from zero the two/three children[109] under the pretexts of high costing per

---

105. Harari, *Homo Deus*, 272, "Ask a teacher—whether in kindergarten, school or college—what she is trying to teach. '.. above all I try to teach them to think for themselves.'"

106. Harari, *Homo Deus*, 263, "Today people marry for love, and it is their personal feelings that give value to this bond. Hence, if the very same feelings that once drove you into the arms of one man now drive you into the arms of another, what's wrong with that?"

107. Marsden, *The Twilight of American Enlightenment*, xxii, "One of the most conspicuous continuity with the eighteenth century and discontinuity with the twenty-first century was in assumptions regarding male leadership."
Shapiro, *Primetime Propaganda*, 88, "... comedy has always mocked fathers—fathers are familial stand-ins for the social authority structures."

108. Harpur, *God Help Us*, 31, "Reality in moral conduct as well as anywhere else is what we choose to make it, they insist." 41, "The nub of the matter, however, is the avoidance of causing pain to others by word or deed."

109. McKibben, *Falter*, 10–11, "Women, with more education and at least a modicum of equality, have gone from having more than five kids apiece on the average in

In the West Vertically

child, excess world populations, and freedom from encumbering parental duties. With regard to the second excuse, overpopulation and fears of starvation, many prevent conception and/or in abortuaries kill basic consequences of human sexuality. The whole dereliction of society's backbone responsibilities, of course, popularized since the sexual revolution of the 1960s anti-family cultures across the West, further illustrates the covetousness of individualism, also within radicalized minority groupings.

Making matters worse, domestically violent men kill women.[110] Husbands, boyfriends, partners in fury or out of desperation slay wives, mothers, daughters, sisters, friends, and colleagues; femicides occur in statistically sufficient numbers to make women look askance at men in socially and economically fraught circumstances; for marginalized, deranged, and financially cornered men drive fearing-for-safety women and children into shelters, one available resource of safety. These private ordeals burst infrequently into public tragedies, a fractured murder-suicide relationship of highly prominent Westerners, for instance. The unknown annual body count shows the end to which many of this civilization misconstrue and mismanage maleness, thereby ruining the societal nerve centers, marriages/families.

By destroying the integrity of nuclear family life in whatever way, Western deities exude a contagious self-loathing, allegedly refusing to bring children into this ugly and cruel world, which the people of other civilizations do not share. Westerners now in kneejerk fashion, without a second thought, do as the larger-than-life gods and goddesses: bound in dreams of cosmopolitanism they refuse to build up the Caucasian population, fearing racist accusations and shaming white privilege. Hence they commit to abortion and childlessness.

Because marriage and family remain social premises, Westerners more than ever blend into fluid structures that resemble marital units as cohabitation and as groupings in temporarily shared common space. These come and go in the pursuit of satisfying lusts and needs. Such centers of things now replace marriages/families to discover in an unfamiliar,

---

1970 to having fewer than two and a half today, probably the most rapid and remarkable demographic change the planet has ever witnessed."

110. Streissguth, *Hate Crimes*, 141, misogyny: "The aversion to the opposite sex, most often to denote sexism by men against women (the aversion of women to men is known more specifically as misandry)."

65

individualistic, and uncaring world some awareness of invisible hands that promise belonging and love, no matter how pathetic.[111]

Bottom Tier Heroism

When the significance of the Greek and Roman deities faded from Western consciousness, ancients in old Europe fantasized other heroes into existence. Men emulated as role models those heroes—frequently in warrior mode: King Arthur and his Round Table or the Knights of the Crusades—role models that made women swoon in the strong arms of masculinity. Typically, the champions of past heroic visions perished too, now only evident in dust-covered literature or trapped in fairy tales. Literary students of Western origins find those past heroes and even heroines interesting character studies.

Role models fascinate. Since the throes of the 2019—2022 pandemic the people of the West idealize a new breed, frontline workers and first responders, men and women who knowingly risked life and limb assisting others in critical situations, even those deathly ill with the Covid-19 virus and its variants or who overdosed multiple times on opioids. This hero-worship now in every present finds figures to admire and inspire, even if too poor for deification, elevation to the Top Tier.

Predominant in the West, however, are disposable heroized and deified sports figures, movie stars, and financial magnates, glitterati gods and goddesses, who inspire all of the Bottom Tier with covetous meaningfulness.

Bottom Tier Aging

Westerners fashionably push the elderly aside, into retirement communities or nursing homes, each person a spent force.[112]

Settling into a retirement home comes with a measure of cooperation, a searching for the golden years with like-minded retirees; in this voluntary self-isolation, the wealthier—within gated communities—unite into favorable commitments that allegedly proffer the delights of superannuation.

---

111. Harari, *Homo Deus*, 263, "The most interesting discussions in humanist ethics concern situations like extramarital affairs, when human feelings collide."

112. Harari, *Homo Deus*, 57, "A friend once told me that what she fears most about growing old is becoming irrelevant, turning into a nostalgic old woman who cannot understand the world around her, or contribute much to it."

Here gerontologists work with death-defying hopes to give longevity better definitions.

Distinctly different from retirement communities, nursing homes provide involuntary isolation necessitated by ill-health, dementia, loneliness, and inability through enfeeblement to provide basic care, also to free adult children from the daily chores necessary for aging parents. Enclosure in nursing homes comes at a critical time, there to face in benign neglect the end of life traumas. For these *retirees* Western governments and corporate interests create hospital-like settings and infirmaries to house now burdensome men and women no longer valuable to the larger community. This out-of-sight/out-of-mind mentality, except for immediate family, reveals a major, major blemish in Western society. For once through the front doors of such establishments care deteriorates, amidst inconsolable fears of gerontophobia.

Deteriorating care in nursing homes came into public light at the beginning of the Covid-19 pandemic, each home a composite of mismanagement factors—poorly trained and ill-paid staff, patient abuse, dwindling social contacts, worn-out equipment, in short, deficiencies in basic managing and nursing. Sudden guilt levels in government offices and surviving children's hearts briefly upgraded concerns for loved ones and commitments to finance care.

For the moment, *invisible* nursing home residents find that instead of dying in fast-forward MAiD institutions, they live longer on medical maintenance and interesting nutrition, centenarians no longer demographic oddities; they move the biological clock into new dimensions of longevity.

In Western civilization the elderly whether in retirement communities or in nursing homes find they rate caring attention at the hands of remunerated strangers.

Bottom Tier Vagrancy

Due to chronic unemployment as well as un-employability, overprized housing, malingering addictions, and untreated mental illnesses, chronic homelessness opens up a palpable blight spreading out over Western civilization.[113] Destitution in the lower-income brackets—evidence of social

---

113. Thatcher, *The Downing Street Years*, 146, " . . . welfare arrangements encouraged dependency and discouraged a sense of responsibility, and television undermined common moral values that would once have united working-class communities."

instability—gives way to petty crime, prostitution, vagrancy, and panhandling. Governments, preoccupied with voters' interests, are unwilling and hence unable to perceive the extensive damages vagrants incur to themselves and the communities they aggravate. Low-cost housing, methadone clinics, and emergency measures drain more than privately run soup kitchens and escalate government pensions that ameliorate the descending spiral that drag these men and women, among whom teenagers, into oblivion. Assistance of every kind to manage this caustic Western problem hides the fact that large majorities with detached superiority wish it to fade away with the morning fog, leaving sidewalks, roadways, and parks vagrant-free.

Despite millions upon millions of public funds thrown at homelessness and vagrancy through social agencies, the police, and the courts, these bottom of the Bottom Tier people still (in summer time) sleep in doorways, occupy parks, build tent cities in out-of-the-way spots, crowd sidewalks, and push worldly possessions about in "borrowed" grocery carts. These men and women eventually perish by murder or by overdose. Since they no longer benefit the aristocracy they die lonely in unseen places, with burial at government expense, to be replaced by more equally useless to the Top-Tier gods and goddesses.

Everything about vagrancy irritates Western self-sufficiency, yet Westerners capable of removing the causes of homelessness do so with slipshod measures. At the bottom of the Bottom Tier life is grim, possible only on the left-overs of liberal largesse.

Bottom Tier Anxiety

Throughout Bottom-Tier populations waves of angst, undifferentiated anxiety, isolate individuals by way of disorders, breakdowns, depressions, and addictions. Where community leaders, primarily the aristocracy, fail at radiating substantial hope, worries close-off horizons, then give way to other flaming destructions of the mind. Westerners from the essentially more sensitive down to the incorrigibly selfish peering into the darkness perceive little curative light in the immediate vastness of personal despair, nary a glimmer.

Marsden, *The Twilight of the American Enlightenment*, 3, "Suddenly television was dictating how most people spent their leisure time."

In the West VERTICALLY

- Concerns that immigrants and migrants wear down Caucasian strongholds harden into undefinable angst.
- Communities of color perceive no end to racial profiling[114] and find perilous anxieties immediately beneath the social surface.
- Extreme weather patterns compound undefinable fears.
- Keeping up with industrial and technological inventions awakens insomnia.
- Racism with its violence demeans both sides of the conflict.[115]
- Actualities of wild fires, floods, earthquakes, volcanoes, and insect plagues shred Western confidence at ground level.
- Possibilities of food and water shortages confuse trust in political leadership.
- Poverty marginalizes all on the way down with hopelessness.
- Unemployable people fear depression and its results.[116]
- Aging brings on terrors of uselessness.
- Dangerous levels of indebtedness—personal, industrial, governmental—burden the maxed-out down with alarms of insolvency.
- Fears of pandemics, invisible enemies, haunt young and old alike.

---

114. Morgan, *Australia*, 22, "White Australians had already discriminated against Aborigines on racial grounds since the beginning of European settlement in New South Wales. Asian immigrants posed another type of racial and cultural threat."

Streissguth, *Hate Crimes*, 142, racial profiling: "The selection of members of a certain ethnic group for closer scrutiny by police or other authority figures."

115. Streissguth, *Hate Crimes*, 142, racism: "The doctrine that certain ethnic groups are as a rule inferior or superior to others based on perceived characteristics among members of that group."

Shapiro, *The Authoritarian Moment*, 56, "The system, in other words, is designed to *create* racially disparate outcomes; any proof of racially disparate outcomes is evidence of the malignancy of the system."

116. Ferguson, *The Great Degeneration*, 3, "Unemployment is being concealed—and rendered permanent—in ways all too familiar to Europeans. Able-bodied people are classified as disabled and never work again."

Saul, *The Unconscious Civilization*, 13, " . . . about 10%. This has not moved down seriously for a decade. This is also an unfinanceable level of exclusion for any society. In other words, no society can afford to lose the productivity of 10% of its population over an extended period of time."

Furthermore, escalating anxieties raise doubts about community well-being, family solidarity, and health provisions, each of which exasperates chronic pain, protracts disability, damages security, and hesitates to trust government leadership as well as, if not more so, aristocratic modeling. Increases in addiction generate more overwrought angst. Thoughts stray into death by suicide.[117]

Immediately under the Western social surface, rankling turmoil turns citizens down a slow spiral of disquiet into hostile shiftlessness. Fear of the still impenetrable over the immediate horizon generates anguish and torment of soul. Now, from deep down separation anxieties in the back of multiple heads bother about: when will the West's managers turn off the electricity and shut down the flow of oil? Will generation of solar and wind powers be sufficient? What happens when the manufacturing and smuggling of opioids and barbiturates cease? Anxiety spawns accursed apprehensions.

Bottom Tier Humor

Stand-up comics, late-night TV hosts, and cartoonists humor the inane and the anal, human sexuality therein by default a favorite.[118] In banal and ribald ways humorists sarcastically play up political weaknesses, often with the intent to do damage. Such tactless entertainments as irreverent comedy, whether in music, by film, through literature, or with stand-up comics push meaningfulness aside, to prevent reflection on the West's numerous permutations in matters of the soul; bawdy attacks draw attention in unfavorable ways away from the sense of living.[119] In fact, much current comedy drops down into the anal preoccupation of a two-year old, into misogynistic amusement, or into witty one-liners that immediately lose any relevance.[120]

---

117. Proser, *Savage Messiah*, 154, "The bloody goddess Kali began calling on families around the world. In the years between 2000 and 2017, she delivered tens of thousands of corpses to parents. The suicide rate had increased 43 percent among those aged twenty to thirty-five."

118. Marsden, *The Twilight of the American Enlightenment*, 4, ". . . the abruptness of the TV revolution and its revolutionizing impact in changing the lives of almost everyone in the country was something that demanded reflection."

119. Shapiro, *Primetime Propaganda*, 87, ". . . while modern comedy has become more and more nihilistic, it remains a dominant mode on television."

120. Steyn, *Lights Out*, 62, "I would love to see a really great Muslim sitcom. After all, one of the worst forms of discrimination is to exclude someone from the joke."

Jests and jokes reflective of many vulgarizing trends impact only momentarily and perish in spurts of laughter.

Despite the low, low standard of Western humor, one social obligation for every Westerner? A sense of humor, however tasteless, even the silliest joking. Lacking this absurdity diminishes a Westerner's persona.

Bottom Tier Musicality

Top-Tier musical stars determine styles that Bottom-Tier singers/musicians, questing for fame and fortune, copy in complimentary and competitive ways. The intention of Western music-making is simple enough: to magnify Top-Tier aristocrats through 1) purchasing their musical productions, by 2) duplicating their styles in order also in this way to venerate the aristocracy, and 3) stop reflecting on the fragile evidence of religiosity. Except for seasonal adjustments, around Christmas and Easter, only then do the aristocrats' paid managers and handlers allow in the spirit of pagan festivals songs of religiosity. On the whole attention now falls, never accidentally, on Valentine's Day, Mother's Day, Father's Day, and Hallowe'en. Top-Tier personages refuse to tolerate any imbalance—all for them and none for others—to which communal order Westerners happily and sheepishly bow.

In its many types and modes, Western music and song voice aspects of and stimulate its mother culture. Whether directly committed to exalt the aristocracy or indirectly through western, rock, rap, pop or even classical traditions, every style binds the attention of Westerners to this-world's gods and goddesses along with the money that they titillatingly hold out in tempting ways. Whether mournful, hopeful, or painful each musical mood circumvents consideration of this civilization's common failures and fashionable vices, lest any or many perceive over the edge swarthy specters of fallacy lying in wait. Even in dilettante forms—background noise, humming, or karaoke sing-alongs—the always alluring voice of the Western heart comes alive, leading multitudes of the unwary into its enclosure of nothingness. Mindless popular music/song ensembles that distract or classical music that require focused attention inspires singers and listeners sensitive to the Western soul to express its matters of the heart.[121] As such, musical compositions from the ditty to the orchestral symphony reach deep

---

121. Harari, *Homo Deus*, 302, "Beauty is in the ears of the listener, and the customer is always right."

into and confirm the emotive powers of what it means to be a Westerner. The whole of Western musicality, for sure, keeps attention away from the Christ and his Kingdom.

Western music and song up all decibels and down every chord trivialize the hyperbolic worth of this civilization and, more, of its numerous citizens. Specifically in its money-making potentials and promises of the easy life among the aristocrats, many find a singing career on secular wavelengths the passion of life, worthwhile every sacrifice.

Bottom Tier Pornography[122]

Human incompetence with sexuality demands compensational activity, such as pornography,[123] as well as sexually explicit novels, graphic literature, strip clubs, titillating films, and other prurient depictions of men and women in fornicative posturing. As men visually misuse provocatively presented female bodies and women similarly abuse male bodies, pornographers sell the results to more than enough willing publics for embroiling addictions. Instant availability on the Internet, open doors into strip clubs, discreet invitations to private parties, easy entry into "adult" bookshops, and all sorts of magazines with unambiguous photography show up consumers' sexual inadequacies; these Westerners need to feed addictions to achieve unsatisfiable gratification. For whatever taste—cisgender, transgender,[124] sadist, masochist, pederast, homosexual/lesbian, and dozens more—these obscenities cater to every consuming taste.

What appeals to many grownups fearful of marital sexuality is pederasty, men "loving" boys, and adults obsessed with "kiddie porn," to satisfy altered perceptions of harm to children. Such lust smites children, even babies, with ruinous exploitation. Cruelly twisted longings at brutalizing levels of desperation drive pornographically infatuated Western adults into fearful judgment.[125]

122. Dreher, *Live Not By Lies*, 44, "Ours is also an intensely sensual age, one that emphasizes sensate experiences over spiritual and rational ideals."

123. Boyd, *Canadian Law*, 17, "Pornography is seen by some radical feminists as worthy of censorship and criminalization—as the embodiment of the male abuse of women."

124. Fukuyama, *Identity*, 8, "Sudden attention was paid to transgender people, who had previously not been recognized as a distinct target of discrimination."

125. Ferguson, *Doom*, 238, "In the period between 1957 and 2020, the United States—and the world— faced only one historically significant pandemic, and that was

Toleration of and participation in pornographic lusts ruin at every level men-women marriage-bonds, the one sex dehumanizing the other or the same sexes each other.

Bottom Tier Addiction

More Westerners, starting with marijuana and social drinking, seek recourse in addictive substances to escape tensions of boredom,[126] physical pain, mental anguish, unrequited love, bullying peer pressure, and even the idleness of the lazy. These ruthless urges, of course, depend on access to governmental injection sites, doors into beer/liquor outlets, and the availability of illicit dealers. Beginning with social drugs—purely for pleasure— far too many dependencies end in hell holes, the inevitability of substance abuse. These heedlessly lost ways of life characterize the West not only on the Bottom-Tier bottom among the homeless and other social rejects who survive on street drugs.

Mounting emergency services for alcohol abusers and opioid-related overdosers indicate multiple horrors of the deadly dependencies. Moreover, increasing demands for and availability of alcohol and drugs make such dependencies a scandal of agonizing proportions, for relatives of addicts perhaps more so. Western authorities in every country show a lack of will applicable to these crises For libertarians the better way to end wars on drugs is surrender, thus resolving high rates of imprisonment, fatherlessness, crime, cartel activity, overdosings, and budget deficits. This opens site doors from which addicts and even madmen emboldened by government moneys stumble about in Western communities.

Nevertheless, for release from pain and to simplify hurts of disappointment the abuses of "anesthetics" testify to the irresistible hungers for which many surrender all.[127] Whether a beverage, powder, or pill, these forms of healing kill, for victims—barring a minority—find they are unable

---

the one caused by HIV and the lethal disease it can lead to, acquired immunodeficiency syndrome (AIDS)."

126. Marsden, *The Twilight of the American Enlightenment*, xxxviii, "In the midst of affluence, 'America is said to have the highest per capita boredom of any spot on earth.'" This boredom "encases" the West.

127. Hedges, *America*, 84, "Those who seek to anesthetize themselves, to retreat into the underworld of Lotus-eaters, are attempting to flee from pain, despair, and dislocation. They seek in opioids the affirmation, warmth, and solidarity that should come from families, friends, and communities where they can find purpose and dignity."

to extricate themselves from the entangling grasp of painkillers, at least not without well-schooled outside sources.

Making matters worse, unscrupulous medical practitioners—sociopathic in the quest for Top-Tier wealth—with god-like powers prescribe painkillers indiscriminately; operators of such "pill mills" push enslavements along until death swallows down town drunks, back-alley derelicts, and others, people higher up in the Bottom and Top Tiers. Meanwhile, governments pass on the perennially increasing costs of these cravings to taxpayers by withdrawing the moneys from public funds for bogus prescriptions, injection sites, and funeral services for derelicts—evidence of liberal progressiveness.

Liquor stores, beer outlets, marijuana boutiques, and injection sites along with ready availability of intoxicants in homes, bars, and restaurants ease ingesting painkillers, love potions, and social lubricants. Innumerable across Western civilization find themselves impotent to cope alone with the temperamental outcomes of popular, licit or illicit, self-medications—alcohol and opioids tainted with fentanyl and carfentanil—possibly also laced with barbiturates, adding to these benodiasepine/norfludiasepam, or benzos, apparently one of the latest available super-killers. With bureaucratically controlled applications for medical marijuana licenses and the handiness of this substance still on the black market, Westerners on the whole indicate addictive dependencies stronger than caffeine and nicotine that sweep aside the Western reputation for stability and virility. Too many require artificial supports to get through the day, to say nothing of the night. This reliance on addictives carries Western civilization away, onto and over the edge into unexplored social cataclysms.

Public revulsions with respect to addiction, police warnings about its horrors, and public health officials' alarms, nothing seems to curb these social enemies; broken bodies for coffin fillers exceed burial parties. Still the carnage on the roads, grief to families, injury to addicts, and cost to overcrowded emergency wards raise the specter of dependency to most concerning levels, even mitigating the will to live.

In conjunction with the poisonous interests of addiction, huge money-making businesses and enormous taxation benefits accrue massive benefits from growing/manufacturing, marketing, and distributing addictives. Even the sight of broken bodies, delusional minds, suffering families, and overburdened emergency units never seem to raise social guilt levels to confound and eliminate addictions.

The production of illicit drugs, from cocaine for partying to deadly fentanyl to deadlier carfentanil, and benzos for easing pain, along with consuming alcoholic beverages help uncountable Westerners to cope with emptiness of soul or relax moral commitments. Life-endangering escapes from the realities of living draw in always more of the reckless and unwary.[128]

Bottom Tier Religiosity

For the people of the West Auguste Comte philosophically envisioned a religion-less, and hence godless, civilization as the light for the world. This vision, laden down with humanistic ideals and overflowing with scientific methodologies, had to carry Westerners to glorious heights of self-assured autonomy. To make this happen, beginning in Europe, Westerners had to direct each other in the admiration of human goodness and jealously protect each other for attaining the free-thinking era. Comte thus elevated the Renaissance's imposing presence first to Enlightenment loftiness.[129]

To activate the socialization of this philosophical ideal Comte with arrogant confidence outlined the way now civilization-wide believed, that is, the inexorable movement from a theological state of things through believing metaphysical eternals into a purely scientific mode of life. He assumed that in the not distant future from 1798–1857 that the people of the West had to progress resolutely into this atheistic reality, atheistic Europe leading.[130] The ruling class over this coming world order taking shape among cosmopolitan aristocrats tolerated pointless religiosities temporarily, for Western deities each such anti-humanist madness wastages of time and breakages with progressivism. This conviction of a scientific super-mode of reality grew with steady determination through processes of political enactments, educational policies, and social media punditry.

---

128. Performance-enhancing drugs better qualify men and women for sports, entering competitions as superhuman beings; they imagine themselves not unlike gods and goddesses while ignoring the destructiveness of these legal and semi-legal anabolic steroids. They build up a false self-esteem and a pretentious reputation based on incriminating evidence.

129. Saul, *The Unconscious Civilization*, 35, "For the moment, I would like to expand on the particularity of gods, kings and groups. They cannot function happily within a real democracy—that is, within a society of individuals."

130. Harpur, *God Help Us*, 53, " . . . reading modern physicists today, one might be astonished at their new-found interest in eastern and western forms of mysticism, and at their willingness to speculate about metaphysics (that which lies beyond the physical)."

Self-Examination

\/

Western people tolerate the religiosities the Renaissance marginalized—Roman Catholicism, Anglicanism/Episcopalianism, and Protestantism, the latter refurbished in America as Evangelicalism/Dispensationalism.[131] Even while the Renaissance assumed domination, at first Protestantism and Roman Catholicism, then also Anglicanism/Episcopalianism, gained gigantic profiles, numerically and vocally enough to trouble the developing humanism.

These merit-earning entities display enough common ground with Westernism, specifically Renaissance philosophy, in order not to irritate governing gods and goddesses overmuch. Whether Roman Catholic, Anglican/Episcopalian, or Evangelical, each strives for self-righteousness, the self-esteem that refracts the spirit of the West sufficiently to escape ostracism or such persecution as now common in the Middle East and the Far East (China in particular). Therefore these old-time religiosities on the basis of a family resemblance receive a measure of acceptance. This is to say, Roman Catholics, Anglicans/Episcopalians, and Protestants carry within themselves the self-esteem/self-righteousness acceptable on a timeline by which to disappear. Roman Catholic acceptance is based on Semi-Pelagianism, Anglican/Episcopalian as well as Protestant acceptance on Arminianism.[132] The fundamental flaw in Semi-Pelagianism and equally in Arminianism—self-righteousness: self-esteem merited by good deeds that reflect the West's spirit and mollify its boss-people enough—recommends that each of the Renaissance's religious left-overs receive a measure of toleration, provided none lingers long on the frayed welcome matt and none gathers undue notoriety in social media.

---

131. Packer and Howard, *Christianity*, 17, "In the United States a conversionist folk religion (legalistic, biblicist, revivalist, conservative, credulous, anti-cultural, authoritarian) has in the past been strong."

132. Following in the Roman Catholic pattern: Packer, *A Quest for Holiness*, 127–128, " . . . the Arminians drew two deductions: first, that since the Bible regards faith as a free and responsible human act, it cannot be caused by God, but is exercised independently of him; second, that since the Bible regards faith as obligatory on the part of all who hear the gospel, ability to believe must be universal. Hence, they maintained, Scripture must be interpreted as teaching the following positions: (1) Man is never so completely corrupted by sin that he cannot savingly believe the gospel when it is put before him, nor (2) is he ever so completely controlled by God that he cannot reject it. (3) God's election of those who shall be saved is prompted by his foreseeing that they will of their own accord believe."

In the West VERTICALLY

On account of Western estimation governed by the Renaissance, the Enlightenment, and Modernism, the religiosities' questing efforts to snatch sinners away from the jaws of a non-existent hell may seem innocuous at best or, worse, annoy the aristocracy. And the aristocratic gods and goddesses on the Top Tier prefer not to be annoyed. They have prescribed the way to become perfectly good people by way of humanism, and consider the religiosities, except for the accommodating self-righteousness, disobedient to the Western spirit; these religiosities must show they are in and of the West enough to be acceptable. Moreover, as the three left-over religiosities openly assume places of control in Western territories, they hereby walk down the migratory order circumspectly into the native core of godlessness. At the same time ecclesial leaders unobtrusively dumb-down for membership original theological, ethical, and behavioral standards. The aristocracy with profuse Bottom-Tier support prefers in the mass media only the lowest common denominator celebrations—Valentine's Day, Mother's Day, Father's Day, and Hallowe'en—or mockery of conservative denominations to inflame fundamentalists. As the religiosities, even the conservative, conform to the secular world in order to experience community with the world, ostensibly to influence the culture of the day, each becomes flavorless salt best thrown away.[133] Under the West's blanket condemnation the Gospel suffers, the offense of the Cross much too much to bear.

In addition to Roman Catholicism, Anglicanism/Episcopalianism, and Protestantism, several homegrown religiosities sprouted in the West, eighteenth-century Mormonism, Jehovah's Witnesses, and Christian Science, and twentieth-century Pentecostalism, each thick with self-righteousness sucked from the desolate soils of Western civilization. As domestic plants these religiosities manage with human ingenuity to convince and convict themselves of merited righteousness that makes them acceptable among the mercurial ranks of the gods and goddesses. Separately, these religiosities adopt inhospitable frameworks of thinking, feeling, and acting to prevent any other sort of light to penetrate the darkness within each, the Gospel specifically. Journeying according to the migratory order into the depths from which they sprouted, each demands the right of way at the expense of the others, naturally the Religion also.

After the Second World War other religiosities emerged in the West more boldly either through the fecundity of internal growth or over migratory routes as immigrants—Judaism, Hinduism, Buddhism,

---

133. Hedges, *America*, 32, "Reality has been converted into image and stagecraft."

Mohammedanism, New Ageism, Wicca, Baha'ism, Falun Gong, for now to mention these only. By endorsing pertinent social/political goals these alien philosophies multiply on bases of Western largesse and naiveté. Over a generation or two, obeying the migratory order, the children of these religiosities assume Western dress, languages, and foods as they integrate into the West's sorry spectacles of spiritual barrenness.[134]

\/

Religiosities constrained by multiculturalist strictures inevitably jostle each other in badly organized mixtures of political correctness to push for more space,[135] until one with sufficient clout dominates all. That domination then determines the tyranny of the day, unlike any totalitarianism operative now in neighboring civilizations.[136] This tyranny, with implanted microchips and transcranial stimulators, refuses to make the errors of deceased dictators. The coming dictatorship rejects present-day China, Iran, and North Korea's regimes, and even the Taliban's caliphate dreams, as mere playgrounds.

Roman Catholicism

After its marginalization by the Renaissance, Roman Catholicism by incremental steps turned into a decisive force throughout the West, political leaders by turn kissing the ruling pope's ring to indicate submission. By competing foremost against Anglicanism/Episcopalianism, Protestantism, and then also the homegrown as well as immigrant religiosities, its mere existence denies the rationalism so vigorously impressive in the Enlightenment and in Modernism, apparently now even surviving the basic tenets of Postmodernism. In its elaborate organizational structuring and sophisticated networking of philosophical schools, Thomism still leading, the historical facticity of Roman Catholicism continually answers one of

---

134. Ferguson, *Civilization*, 289, "Worse, this spiritual vacuum leaves West European societies vulnerable to the sinister ambitions of a minority of people who do have religious faith—as well as the political ambition to expand power and influence of that faith in their adopted countries."

135. Harpur, *God Help Us*, 30, " . . . currently there is a growing interest in things of the spirit, an awareness that, however essential a reasonable amount of material prosperity may be, we do not live by bread alone."

136. Proser, *Savage Messiah*, 156, "Teaching the next generation that life is meaningless, truth is unknowable, and that tradition and conventional wisdom must be discarded yields predictable results. Such a corrosive worldview will only produce rotting fruit."

the ultimate life-and-death questions through its Semi-Pelagianism: how to appear fully esteemed before the saints worshiped by the pope of the day. From its earliest roots, post-Renaissance Roman Catholicism drank in enough of the Western spirit to be an acceptable entity, provisionally.

Anglicanism/Episcopalianism

Anglicanism/Episcopalianism, a crossover between Protestantism and Roman Catholicism started in sixteenth-century England, a heavy-handed accomplishment of Henry VIII, 1491–1547. He centered this maladaptation of Roman Catholicism and Protestantism in the See of Canterbury and about the Archbishop of Canterbury, thus replacing Rome and pope with his own inventions. In America, after the 1765–1783 Revolution, Anglicans, to shed the British aura, identified themselves as Episcopalians. In rejecting Roman Catholicism and by distorting Protestantism, Anglicanism/Episcopalianism is neither Roman Catholic nor Protestant. With the solidity of Roman Catholicism and the volatility of Protestantism, the continuing Church of England answers an ultimate question in life and in death with the Protestant variation of Semi-Pelagianism, Arminianism: how are we/am I acceptable to the deities worshiped? Episcopalians exemplify in this self-righteousness enough empathy with the spirit of the West to be tolerated. Since its inception, Anglicanism/Episcopalianism found social esteem among upper classes in all Western countries, in English speaking lands a force to reckon with.

Pietism

Reacting with revulsion to the Enlightenment's rationalism, specifically developing Neo-Scholasticism, Pietists stressed emotions, conviction, and prayer rather than doctrines and intellectual assent to creedal statements. These people agreed with the Churches' historical confessions, true, but generated little interest in the doctrinal teachings of the Scriptures, at least not rationalistic definitions. Pietists wanted evidential reformation of soul, conversion, and love as the ruling guide in life individually and congregationally. The New Testament's moral standard brought about warm, deep religious experiences as confirmation of Christianity.

Pietism resented theological strife, pursued unity, and encouraged expression, always within the soul of Romanticism.

Protestantism

Since its sixteenth-century origin, Protestantism in its impressive genius opposed Roman Catholicism and adopted the rationalism of the Renaissance relative to Arminianism, a doctrine cherished by its mainline churches and nourished with equal intensity in smaller denominations. By submitting to the Renaissance's rationalism, denominationally ministers and members fear the five Reformation strengths—*sola scriptura, sola fide, sola gratia, sola Christo,* and *sola Gloria Deo*—by answering an ultimate question in life and death in the Arminian manner; they dreaded and dread foundational trust in the grace the Christ revealed on the Cross. Compliant with the spirit dominant in Westernism, Protestants compromised; they adopted Arminianism, especially the rejection of *sola gratia,* thus conforming to Semi-Pelagianism. According to Arminianism, each person individually and individualistically has to *accept* the Gospel, a work totally dependent on human initiative; this makes faith reliant on a non-existent freedom of the will. Such denial of the Christ's omnipotence and omniscience condemns Protestants' self-righteousness, the whole a tree bearing bad fruit. Such exposure of Protestantism's seamy side makes also this religiosity tolerable to the West, its capricious freedom of the will a made-in-the-West article of faith.[137] More of the prejudices and shortcomings of Protestantism[138] appear in its predisposition to divide—Lutheran, Adventist, Anabaptist, Methodist, Moravian, Pentecostal, Quaker, Mennonite, Hutterite;[139] etc.—that contributes to mocking this religiosity. Moving predominantly among the Bottom-Tier's lower classes, Protestantism grew numerically and powerfully in denial of Comte's arrogant theology>metaphysics>science schematics.

---

137. Harari, *Homo Deus*, 261, "For centuries' humanism has been convincing us that we are the ultimate source of meaning, and that our free will is therefore the highest authority of all. Instead of waiting for some external entity to tell us what's what, we can rely on our own feelings and desires." 327, "Liberals value individual liberty so much because they believe that humans have free will."

138. Marsden, *The Twilight of the American Enlightenment*, xxvii, " . . . [Protestantism in the public arena] fostered an informal Protestant establishment, or privileges for mainstream Protestants in public life, there were always those who were less privileged, who were excluded or discriminated against—such as Catholics, Jews, people of other world faiths, or those in smaller sectarian groups."

139. Quakers, Mennonites, Hutterites, etc., find that pacifist ideals fill out sufficiently the necessary requirements for self-righteousness.

Mormonism

Mormonism in its international format interprets Christian particularities mainly by way of Joseph Smith's, 1805–1844, anti-trinitarian *Book of Mormon*, a work structured by and riddled with the man's inventiveness. Now consolidated as the Church of Jesus Christ of Latter-day Saints headquartered in Salt Lake City, Utah, this global phenomenon by its clean living and missionary work appeals to each person's self-esteem, the whole rendering a good people tolerated in the West. With its modern Modernism and by its eccentricities, as the baptism of the dead, Mormonism in the name of its god(s) gains numerous adherents, huge voting blocs in every Western country.

Jehovah's Witnesses/Russellism

Now a global religiosity with pronounced millenarian beliefs, its members, predominantly petit bourgeoisie, endorse a self-righteousness typically Western. Members compete for placement among the 144,000 true believers mentioned in the biblical *Book of Revelation*. They find that spurious interpretations of the Kingdom of God as mediated through Watchtower publications solve all problems international as well as personal.

Christian Science

Initiated by Mary Baker Eddy, 1821–1910, and her *Science and Health With Key to the Scriptures*, Christian Science still attempts to accomplish a biblical command Jesus addressed to his twelve disciples—partial Matthew 10:8, "Heal the sick, raise the dead, cleanse lepers, cast out demons." Christian Science places heavy affirmation on faith healing. The organization itself tends to be secretive—membership by invitation only and after thorough vetting, with accomplishments of miracles the aspirational evidence of self-righteousness, wealth another. In its secretiveness Christian Science stands apart as a luxury brand. Members who succeed in *successful* healings by virtue of this effort find they have earned this religiosity's righteousness, a state of being accomplished by works.

Judaism

During the Roman occupation of the Eastern Mediterranean land bridge and upon the destruction of Jerusalem Jewish remnants moved everywhere searching for safety to escape persecution, the most recent the experiences of the Nazi-inspired Holocaust. After World War Two, expanding Jewish enclaves in the West for now ensure peace and growth, particularly for Talmudism.

Hinduism

With roots receding in deep time, beyond BC 4,000, this religiosity drew into itself many now nameless traditions and philosophies, the whole blending into a henotheism, a pantheon of many gods and goddesses overruled by Brahman, the dominant deity. This Brahman gathers into itself numerous paths of people searching for entry into the eternal bliss of the absolute soul, Nirvana. Hindus believe that through helping others into Nirvana, participating in many feasts, and reincarnating they attain to that self-awareness that earns them total spiritual enlightenment. The religiosity of this ethno-centric stereotype determinedly holds its numerous many away from the Gospel.

Buddhism

Buddhists, through processes of reincarnation, by doing good strive for entry into the delight of Nirvana, the extinction of life. Originating from within Hinduism as a reform movement, penniless Gautama Buddha's invention comprises various traditions, beliefs, and practices branching out into Theravada and resurging Mahayana variants. Following the Four Noble Truths to overcome suffering, Buddhists find they transcend desire and ignorance, which living over many reincarnations opens up into the Buddhist variant of ceaseless bliss, eventually delivering true believers from the will and the desire that produce suffering. With concepts of self-cultivation to achieve both physical and spiritual health Buddhists move on, Nirvana the destination.

Mohammedanism

This seventh-century political eruption bundled largely legal aspects of the Christian Scriptures with many Arabian superstitions to shape monotheistic Islam, the people of which follow Mohammed's five pillars to achieve high standing in self-righteousness—*Shahada, Salah, Zakat, Sawn,* and *Hajj*; with slavish subservience publically identifiable Muslims try to gain Islam's male-dominated heaven. Men who die in holy wars more than by doing Mohammedan's four other pillars earn entry into a remarkably hedonistic and misogynistic paradise.

In the twentieth century Islam spawned Islamism, murderously intense Wahhabism, a fundamental anti-Western extremism with the goal to form in each country an internal caliphate governed by sharia law.[140]

Sikhism

A militant blend of Hinduism and Mohammedanism was born in the Kashmir region, late fifteenth, early sixteenth century, to prevent absorption into either conflictive religiosity, the monotheism of the one and the many deities of the other. An aggressive people, Sikhs own the Mohammedan drive to dominate.

New Ageism.

This twentieth-century phenomenon of diverse beliefs and practices in a highly eclectic structure drew inspiration from old occult traditions and

---

140. Ferguson, *Civilization*, 289, "In reality, the core values of Western civilization are directly threatened by the brand of Islam espoused by terrorists like Muktar Said Ibrahim, derived as it is from the teachings of the nineteenth-century Wahbabist Sayyid Jamal al-Din and the Muslim Brotherhood leaders Hassan al-Banna and Sayyid Qutb."
Harari, *Homo Deus*, 313, "Radical Islam poses no serious threat to the liberal package, because for all their fervour the zealots don't really understand the world of the twenty-first century, and have nothing relevant to say about the novel dangers and opportunities that new technologies are generating all around us."
Steyn, *Lights Out*, 39, "In Europe, it's demography that's ushering in the Islamification of a continent."
Mishra, *Bland Fanatics*, 41, " . . . millions of Muslims, many of them with bitter experiences of authoritarian states, coexist frictionlessly and gratefully with regimes committed to democracy, freedom of religion and equality before the law." 43, "Liberal spaces within Europe have brought many more Muslim women out of their old confinements."

built upon speculative insights from Emanuel Swedenborg, 1688–1772, Franz Mesmer, 1734–1815, spiritualism, theosophy, and marijuana to form the 1960s counterculture, in part identified by sexual permissiveness, to find on earth a holistic life. For this life the doing was more reliable than the believing.[141]

Neo-Paganism

1) Wicca's 1960s witchcraft movement *modernized* paganism's core beliefs, principles, and living styles to construct an updated dark culture of unpredictable powers. Wicca adepts worship a god and goddess, duo-theistically, and fear a horned god, Satan. The gods and goddesses in this satanic haunt demand absolute submission in order to enjoy the life of Wicca. Allegedly a benevolent religiosity, its darkness draws many who have spurned the West's traditional Protestant and Roman Catholic worshiping movements.

2) Neo-Druidry encompasses Westerners who have forsaken Roman Catholicism and Protestantism to find benefaction and worthiness, Druid-fashion, in long rejected Indo-European, Irish, Teutonic, and Greek polytheistic deities. In its pantheon fallacies as the Roman *Fortuna*, Celtic *Morrigan*, Indo-European *Taranis*, Greek *Hermes*, and Greek *Dionysius* keep house, thus to provide nature worshipers with spiritual connections in the universe. By gatherings in groves and at pan-pagan solstice festivals—inclusive, pluralistic, and experiential—druids through offerings by fire discover awing bonds with and personal relations to the natural world, reacting to nature in ways that Westerners allegedly lost. In the polytheism of neo-pagan religiosity Druids search for connections with environmental realities.

Baha'ism

This religiosity finds all religions of essential worth; its true believers follow seven normative paths to a unified world order and government premised on an orderly and progressive way divinely manifested. Obedience

---

141. Shapiro, *Primetime Propaganda*, 32, "On a societal level, . . . disenchantment with American's military foray combined with the sexual revolution, the civil rights movements, the drug subculture, and the growing socialist movement on college campuses to form a powerful counterculture."

to this divine manifestation and its ways finds for Baha'ists a worthwhile destination.

Falun Gong/Falun Dafa

Relatively new and politically right-wing, members of this religiosity of the Dharma Wheel fleeing persecution in China migrate also into the West, from here to oppose Chinese dictatorship.[142] Falun Gong people hold high philosophical standards drawn from religiosities as Buddhism and Taoism.

Astrologism

Longings to ascertain day-by-day the future of individuals, societies, and nations makes spellbound Westerners of all ages and persuasions meditate on the signs of the Zodiac and live by horoscopes. Already ancient Babylonian and Egyptian stargazers promoted this pseudo-science with claims of divine import. Astrologers even now interpret astronomical events involving sun, moon, and stars with predictive meanings cleverly arranged, loading these variant conjectures into the patterns of the stars and unusual conjunctives—eclipses—with compulsions to choose, decide, and act.

Many Westerners otherwise sound of mind compulsively follow astrological pseudo-studies of celestial objects, which signs of the heavens prescribe and proscribe daily activities and recommend irrational decisions, thus giving restless mobility to forces at work based on external powers. Through horoscopy, astrologers gather followers who willingly divide the West according to the Zodiac in order to exploit wealth production, love affairs, business strategies, personal capabilities, or they initiate compromises to shape days and lives for governing, economizing, and existing.

---

142. Manthorpe, *Claws of the Panda*, 14, "The breadth and intensity of the CCP's campaign to exert pressure on immigrants in Canada from China and its possessions, such as Tibet and Xinjiang, has grown in recent years as Canada has become an increasingly popular destination." 20, "Falun Gong members were purged, and many thousands have been imprisoned and killed. The CCP continues to regard the group as one of the main threats to its rule, in part because the Falun Gong leader, Li Hongzhi, now lives in the United States."

Humanism

Throughout Renaissance>Enlightenment>Modernism>Postmodernism revolutionizing the search for meaning evolved most prominently into humanism, the worship of people, thus to find the sense of political, artistic, and religious working. This worship of humanity, an abstraction, leaves everyone free to fill out personal obeisance in the libertarian way before the Western pantheon.[143]

Wokeism[144]

Currently a favorite for Western gods and goddesses, this religiosity perverts humanism into a collective of minority groups for power-mongering; such projections of power through anti-colonizing communities of people mobilize to destroy above all white supremacy,[145] Caucasians allegedly guilty of racializing and suppressing communities of color. These communities of color as communities wield the communist hammer to exercise revolutionary powers, wherewith to destroy the West. Woke-revolutionaries tend to silence and then eliminate Westerners, first conservatives,[146] by fearsome shaming techniques. Through wealth, power, intersectionality, and ethnic partiality Woke-people intend to dominate Western civilization through identity politics, prioritizing diversity over merit. Overcoming racism, these minorities will no longer be silenced, no longer be invisible,

---

143. Harpur, *God Help Us*, 30, "While religious institutions are obviously in a state of decline, the number of men and women in our society who hunger for an authentic spirituality—a framework of thought, words, feelings, and actions that articulates their awareness of being more than consumers or mere ciphers—is rapidly increasing." 31, "Spirituality and the development of one's inner life takes time and discipline." "True spirituality bears the fruit of greater compassion, tolerance, and personal maturity."

144. Shapiro, *The Authoritarian Moment*, 81, "[Wokeism represents] an entire *religious*, unfalsifiable worldview. To deny an inequality means an inequity has taken place became sinful and dangerous: by suggesting that perhaps inequality resulted from luck, natural imbalances, or differential decision making, you are a *threat* to others, a victim-shamer."

145. White privilege: the compilation of advantages, entitlements, benefits, and choices taken for granted by Caucasians.

146. Shapiro, *The Authoritarian Moment*, 26, "Conservatives were to be treated as outsiders." "Better to lop them off the body politic than allow their poison to fester."

In the West VERTICALLY

no longer be taken for granted, and no longer be disrespected. Through intersectionality they, speaking loudly, intend to own the West.[147]

\/

Several pertinent observations:

First, these religiosities in different ways open each sense of the self to merit that self-righteousness which meets the approval of the deities worshiped.[148] To get to the nub: Western forms of worship are merit systems of salvation, thus fundamentally opposing the Religion.

Second, atheists who seek escape from every religiosity adulate themselves.

And third, the many religiosities, especially humanism, spell out the comprehensive Western religious orientation. That is, every Westerner fits into one of these religiously diverse escape plans from the Religion, to obliterate the Religion.[149]

Reflectively now: this enumeration of multiple religiosities resident in the West, humanism and wokeism included, aims 1) to exhibit that the religious powers in humanity are alive, indeed, furiously thriving to prevent burial under left-wing extremism, and 2) to hector followers of Kant and Comte's projections as the greater fools for following the two ignorant visionaries. As such, the moving and expanding religiosities are changing the Western civilization, giving its gods and goddesses more ways to merge

---

147. Fukuyama, *Identity*, 107, 'Each movement represented people who had up to then been invisible and suppressed; each resented that invisibility and wanted public recognition of their inner worth. So was born what we today label as modern identity politics. Only the term was new; these groups were replicating the struggles and perspectives of earlier nationalist and religious identity movements."

148. Huntington, *The Clash of Civilizations*, 64, "That resurgence has involved the intensification of religious consciousness and the rise of fundamentalist movements. It has thus reinforced the differences among religions."

149. To bury Christianity, seventeenth-century Neo-Scholastics choked off the Reformation. Scholars as Johannes Cockeius, 1603–1669, Hermanus Witsius, 1636–1708, and Gisbertus Voetius, 1589–1676, found the rationalism of that age overwhelming and followed this Neo-Scholasticism through to sidetrack Christianity. The Christian identifiers, the three *Forms of Unity*, except momentarily in 1834, 1886, and 1944, and then only in the Lowlands, rest uneasily as honored antiques in Reformed Churches; the 1561 *Confession of Faith*, the 1563 *Heidelberg Catechism*, and the 1618–1619 *Canons of Dort* live on, nostalgic documents with a hallowed past, leftovers of the Reformation barely surviving in the twenty-first century. The Churches that still recognize the *Forms of Unity* depend on Evangelical support systems.

Broadly now, Westerners, to improve the prospects of civilization, abhor the Faith.

SELF-EXAMINATION

on the other side of the edge into hitherto unknown and pitiless blends of mass grief. Day-by-day through growths in number and commitment the religiosities drive this civilization into tradition-shattering servitudes. These impending transitions happen without histrionics as throes of Postmodernism entangle Westerners in more confusion. How Westerners will experience this tumbling over into tomorrows' heavy facts? For certain, the anger of more intolerant gods and goddesses shall avenge Comte's venturing into godlessness.

With multiculturalism[150] Western authorities superimpose power and control also over essentially anti-Western religiosities constantly entering through currents of immigration and migration.[151] Though the deeply ingrained convictions of such religiosities only temporarily submit to the progressive and cultural engineering dominant in the liberal West, they will break out of multicultural strictures. As these alien to the Western frame-of-mind worshipers submit to elusive gods and goddesses they never surrender distinctive markers of self-worth. Emphatically, the deities they worship never compromise! They will have the West.

For now the religiosities—religious fractures—alive in the West prosper with the sense of place in which to nurture an awareness of destiny that the ego-strength of each faith determines: we are somebody; now give us more space and control. Temporarily they submit to the compartmentalization that is multiculturalism and work for more favors from respective deities, while looking askance at the different forms of believing, lest one or more of the others advance in self-interested standing before the aristocracy. Again, emphatically, no religiosity allows itself to be boxed in, confined by artificial boundaries. Each faith manifestation—given opportunity and temptation—crosses over social and political restraints to break clear of pluralism.

Thus far and for now: Westerners within parameters of toleration endure the presence of the active religiosities; these religiosities have in common with the Western spirit that they everyday sedulously commit to meriting the favor of respective deities by means of good works, the good works that glorify these deities and at the same time identify with the West.

---

150. Fukuyama, *Identity*, 111, "*Multiculturalism* was a description of societies that were de facto diverse. But it also became the label for a political program that sought to value each separate culture and each lived experience equally, and in particular those that had been invisible or undervalued in the past."

151. Steyn, *Lights Out*, 176, "The great strength of 'multiculturalism' is not that it's an argument against the west but that it short-circuits the possibility of argument."

Consequently, all individually and communally live engrossed in pursuits of self-righteousness, that sense of the self the deities reward with hedonistic pleasures of materialism, or mammonism. The basic measure of this self-esteem, self-righteousness, the intolerant deities demand in full from worshipers before granting heavenly eventualities of place among the aristocrats. As long as the Western deities define self-righteousness, the *good* people of the West find anchorage in the soul of the Occident. Gods and goddesses never compromise: measure up, or else. Any other standard of goodness fits poorly, specifically the Religion, despite the avowed pluralist slogan, unity in diversity. And as long as Western deities define self-righteousness, the *good* people of the religiosities rest securely in striving for self-righteousness.

Bottom Tier Gambling

More publicly pervasive than ever, Westerners find wagering entertainment,[152] however vindictive in its destruction of hopes and lives. Gambling in casinos, on racetracks, with lotteries, and through slot machines[153] enslaves many and enriches few. In the background and out of sight, cock-fighting and dog-fighting add to the mix. Betting in its many manifestations panders to this civilization's soul-twisting covetousness.

People of the West find the whole of living a risky venture; from planting crops, purchasing houses, borrowing moneys, competing in sports, to planning for retirement; etc., they premise the whole on uncertainty. Indeterminism is basic to the Western soul.

Gambling in its multifarious and nefarious applications defines some fundamental heart-work within Westernism, a participation in ambiguity.[154] Considering the vast gambling enterprises currently in existence and the many prohibitive wagering forms in the shadows of illegitimacy, this *industry* of the future manufactures fantasies, making money with money on

---

152. Hedges, *America*, 212, "Gambling is about creating illusions."

153. Hedges, *America*, 216, "Slot machines cater, like the games on computers and phones, to the longing to flee from the oppressive world of dead-end jobs, crippling debt, social stagnation, and a dysfunctional political system. They shape our behavior with constant bursts of stimulation."

154. Hedges, *America*, 212, "The adrenaline rush of anticipation, administered in twenty-second bursts, on slot machines reconfigures the human brain over hours, days, weeks, months, and years to create a crippling addiction the industry calls 'continuous gaming productivity.'"

the basis of stupefying promises. Such escapes into dreams within dreams, mad methods of solving immediate insolvency or adding to wealth, entangle Bottom-Tier Westerners with cultural delusions, temptations of aristocratic hungers for sudden and uncontrollable riches.

Bottom Tier Sexuality

Reflective of aristocracy's cascading into sexual crises, Bottom-Tier dwellers with little hesitation fall for the follow-the-leaders mode and also indulge in unquantifiable abuses within and without the marriage institution. Other than publicized exploitation of children, human trafficking, and violent rape, few care about the fornicative activities that callously destabilize the West. As long as oppressive men and oppressed women covetously slave for money and immerse children in the same cupidity, interest in the disruptive and corruptive consequences of verbal, emotional, and physical aberrations of sexuality trouble minimally, unless criminal or sensational in nature.

When news-starved social media find prurient marital breakups and sexual obscenities interesting, they make these crises public. Otherwise, immoralities and infidelities appear as normal in Western living. Men abdicate responsibility. Men objectivize women. Fathers ignore children. Women find men superfluous. With abandon, because the aristocrats and authorities sever sexuality from procreation, arbitrary promiscuities of all sorts identify the West, stern reminders that public curiosity pounces hard on salacious displays of perversity.

Matrimony, once generally welcomed throughout the West, regulated men-women relations, protected women from male abuse, limited cruelties of cohabitation, and quelled rampant prostitution. Vows of commitment structured sexual connectivities. Within family bonds male accountability guarded women and children, husbands/fathers leading, providing, and protecting. As a legal and civil institution, matrimony gained high standing, evidence of the West's civilized life. Only, post-1945, the 1960s revolutionary multitudes find fornicative freedom preferential, a sign of maturity, if not human autonomy.[155]

---

155. Ferguson, *Civilization*, 273, "... the Sixties opened the door to a post-Freudian anti-civilization, characterized by a hedonistic celebration of the pleasures of the self, a rejection of theology in favour of pornography and a renunciation of the Prince of Peace for grotesquely violent films and video games that are best characterized as

In the West Vertically

Now as cohabitation, prostitution, adultery, homosexuality, pederasty, pornography, "kiddie porn," and (no-fault) divorce favor misogyny, men find females and children second-class citizens, each and all available for fornicative satisfactions. As Western history flows further into the twenty-first century, women have fewer protections against perversions and assaults, witness overflowing government provided shelters.

Moved by manly masculinity, men in endless fantasies and cravings for instant gratifications find paganization of sexuality preferable, making sex (again) a merely biological necessity. In such socially accepted perversions, prostitution becomes a male preserve and rape a male prerogative, with decriminalized pedophilia thrown in. These perversities Western leadership deems progressive.

Additionally, social acceptance and legal safeguarding of homosexuality, lesbianism, and dysphoria places LBGTQ+ human beings within the precincts of normalcy. With pride parades and pride months accelerating what not long ago was considered insanity, these sexual connectivities now wave multi-colored flags of aggression. One result? Men and boys, women and girls glance in mirrors and fail to recognize themselves as male or female, self-identifying as the one or the other. In this mismatching more predatory lusts agitate the West, each violation of human sexuality damaging male-female marital relationships. As condemnation of sexual predation moderates, this civilization glosses over abhorrent male-female hostilities.

Within the *progressive* constellation of values, a gender-identity crisis takes top priority. This distinctiveness based on feelings, deeply felt,[156] apart from biological factors of genitalia, proliferates throughout the West. Protected by law, gender speech codes bar any form of verbal discrimination that mocks gender identity and sexual orientation. By prohibiting hate-speech Western governments place limitations on the freedom of speech. Through morally perplexing manipulations, transgendering individuals, often children, decide: I will be what I want to be, man or woman.

Also, equally, exploitative sex-traffickers in most sadistic ways control the bodies of (young) women, and men too, always and only for one purpose, money, wherewith to maintain a lavish lifestyle. By brutalizing

---

'warnography.'"

156. Proser, *Savage Messiah*, 228, quoting a left-wing political source: "First, it is important to point out that gender identity and gender expression are basically a state of being, or in other words, something that cannot be fully explained outside the personal experience of the individual in that state."

the self-esteem of victimized men and women pimps market them alive, forcing prostitutes to sell their bodies in terribly dehumanizing manners. Traffickers have but one goal, never mind the grinding misery of victims; they are totally engaged in the Western way, in which unbridled sexual passions determine contemporary culture in a revolutionizing manner.

Dispensable people have now fewer protections against fornicative perversions and assaults. Legislation that sanctions erotic behaviors and legalizes the permissiveness of the times[157] mollifies follies of exploitation and social evil, placing the West on numerous edges to fall over into further demoralization.

Bottom Tier Politics[158]

Western society in each country evolved into unequal political opposites that grind against each other on the pretext of perpetuating democracy.[159] As the two cumbersome entities, liberal and conservative, in respective countries simultaneously reflect the will of the people, each promotes its vision for the civic good, one leaning left-ward and the other pushing right-ward. Each moves outward from or inward to an invisible, undefinable, and movable epicenter that shifts according to popular biases and preferences. Technically, each enhances the platform of the other. Since the Second World War, both entities in response to social pressuring move into more extreme positions, deceptively to promote the wants of the people.

\/

On the left, liberals/progressives by promoting social and cultural engineering conform Western society to far-left political fire-forces such as *Black Lives Matter*[160] *and wokeism*, while riotous and predatory *Antifa*

---

157. Hedges, *America*, 243, "Sexual degeneracy—narcissists are incapable of love—abounds in a society entranced by causal hook-ups and pornography."

158. For this essay I tend to blend into one entity liberalism, the left, and progressive social policies, recognizing at the same time differences exist. Liberalism identifies with individualism, the left with politics, and the other with social engineering.

159. Hedges, *America*, 17, "Democracy throughout most of the history of the West was an anomaly."

160. Fukuyama, *Identity*, 8, "Resentment at indignities was a powerful force in democratic countries as well. The Black Lives Matter movement sprang from a series of well-publicized police killings of African-Americans in Ferguson (Missouri), Baltimore, New York, and other cities and sought to force the outside world to pay attention to the

shock troops fight extreme right entities.[161] These progressives, in the neoliberal manner, accentuate the democratic mentality, one of, by, and for the people. Such commitment to whatever majorities of voters desire, be that death by abortion for the youngest, death through euthanasia for the eldest, or death by gender for those who fail to conform to parental wishes[162] irrepressibly changes the West from its life-enhancing past; the left, sexually confused, with multicultural ingenuity supports homosexualism, lesbianism, and transgenderism, gender dysphoria alongside heterosexuality, each equally worthy of acceptance. For members of Western societies who refuse honoring marital commitments, governments provide processes of easy and cheap divorce as well as endorse the legitimacy of cohabitation, even prostitution. To the racialized communities of color liberals promise to incite anti-racism,[163] look away as vandals topple long-respected statues, and assist with name-changes to public institutions and streets—allegedly to ease brutalizing memories and allow minorities with left-leaning voices to shout and scream for more political progressiveness. Particularly the left attracts whatever absurdities well up out of the human psyche, even past pagan criminal behaviors for a utopian present.[164] These political types seek stronger standing in opinion polls and do whatever necessary in appealing to voters—social engineering, soft dictatorship, and promises of more liberties, even if these liberties kill. Liberals relentlessly move the West onto and over the edge into what they know not.

Citizens pressed into or persuaded by progressive freedoms through an emerging totalitarianism for a more stable present supposedly create the

---

experience of the victims of seemingly casual police violence."

161. Hedges, *America*, 170, "'The majority of antifa have that victim mentality,' [Scott Seddon a right-wing American Patriot went on, referring to antifascists who advocate property destruction and violence.'" 171, "'They're socialists,' Seddon said, 'they're communists. They're the troubled youth of America who don't want to work. They think the upper one percent should give them everything.'"

162. It may be said: governments that promote or condone death sentences for the vulnerable have passed in legitimacy a point of no return.

163. Hedges, *America*, 19, "We cannot battle racism, bigotry, and hate crimes, often stoked by the ruling elites, without first battling for economic justice."

McKibben, *Falter*, 89, "Race, too, has clearly played an enormous role in driving our political transformation."

164. Hedges, *America*, 242, "The longer this illusion is perpetuated, the more an enraged public turns to demagogues who promise a new utopia and then, once in power, accelerate the assault." 198, "The white racists and neo-Nazis may be unsavory, but they too are victims. They too lost jobs and often live in poverty in deindustrialized wastelands."

SELF-EXAMINATION

greater good. Hence liberals propose a totally revolutionary and civilization-wide community with a lasting pattern of life.[165] This community will then house all left-wing biases[166] that periodically erupt into more roiling political hatreds.[167] Without specifying the actualities of such community living liberals nevertheless press on.

\/

From the right, as much of, by, and for the people as the left, conservatives resist the progressives' social and cultural engineering by moving to extremes opposite the left. Radical conservatives assume white supremacist ideals[168] more as a defensive strategy than an offensive communal ordering. Right-wing people work out of the conviction that socialism,[169]

---

165. Proser, *Savage Messiah*, 159, "The greater the diversity in a community, the fewer the people vote and the less they volunteer, the less they give to charity and work on community projects. In the most diverse communities, neighbors trust one another about half as much as they do in the most homogenous settings."

Marsden, *The Twilight of the American Enlightenment*, xxviii, "Those commitments involve a recognition that people differ in their fundamental loves and first principles, and that these loves and first principles act as lenses through which they see everything else."

166. Streissguth, *Hate Crimes*, 140, bias: "A negative opinion held against a group or individual on the basis of race, color, religion, national origin, etc."

167. Harpur, *God Help Us*, 19, " . . . the reason we oppress one another, wage wars, permit injustice, and defile our only natural home is ultimately a spiritual matter."

168. Hedges, *America*, 53, "Whiteness is a dangerous concept. It is not about skin color. It is not even about race. It is about the self-delusion used to justify white supremacy."

Mishra, *Bland Fanatics*, 52, " . . . to grasp the current homecoming of white supremacism in the West, we need an even deeper history—one that shows how whiteness became, in the late nineteenth century, the assurance of individual identity and dignity, as well as the basis of military and diplomatic alliances."

Shapiro, *On the Right Side of History*, 73, "Those on the political Left are certain that those who oppose them are Nazi-esque monsters hell-bent on domination of individual lives; those on the political Right are certain that the opposite is true."

169. Thatcher, *The Downing Street Years*, 12, "Seen from afar, or above, . . . socialism has a certain nobility: equal sacrifice, fair shares, everyone pulling together. Seen from below, however, it looked very different."

Greenspan, *The Age of Turbulence*, 272, "Although the roots of socialism are secular, its political thrust parallels many religious prescriptions for a civil society, seeking to assuage the anguish of the poor."

liberalism,[170] neo-liberalism,[171] and soft tyranny run the West off the rails and over the edge into ruination.[172]

However motivated, conservatives for all the strenuous resistance against the liberals waste scarce energies; they drag along ten, twenty years behind progressive initiatives, every day yielding to neo-liberal measures that steadily become part of the West's religio-ethical stance. Over the past decades a new generation through college/university education affirms normal the latest revolutionary aberrations.[173] Compelled into oppressive political correctness, conservatives fit into a well-worn analogy: placed into the liberal vehicle conservatives as backseat drivers constantly argue that the car is moving too fast in the wrong direction. This is factual. Once conservatives generally perceived themselves a religious people; now they are as atheistic as liberals. Once conservatives fought feminism; now they follow female leaders as readily as liberals. Once conservatives, or neo-conservatives (socons, best known for conservative spending policies),[174] resisted women's health services and access to government financed abortuaries; now they support at government cost supplying *free* abortifacients as well as paying for medically induced death of unborn children in order to feed the covetousness of the voting public. Once conservatives denied the actualities of climate change;[175] now they realize that the majority of col-

---

170. Hazard, *The European Mind*, xviii, "For a civilization founded on Duty—duty towards God, duty towards the sovereign, the new school of philosophers were fain to substitute a civilization founded on the idea of rights—rights of the individual, freedom of speech and opinion, the prerogatives of man as man and citizen."

171. Dreher, *Live Not By Lies*, xiv-xv, "... liberal democracy is degenerating into something like the totalitarianism over which it triumphed in the Cold War."

172. Dreher, *Live Not By Lies*, 76, "[Big Brother] is monitoring virtually every move you make to determine how to sell you more things, and in so doing, learning how to direct your behavior. In this way, Big Brother is laying the foundation for soft totalitarianism, both in terms of creating and implementing the technology for political and social control and by grooming the population to accept it as normal."

173. Shapiro, *The Authoritarian Moment*, 86, "... over the last twenty years a new generation of academics and administrators has taken power, seeking to 'transform higher education itself into an engine of progressive political advocacy, subjecting students to courses that are nothing more than practical training in progressive activism.'"

174. McKibben, *Falter*, 13, "Every economic assumption our governments makes about the future requires doubling the size of the economy again, and then again, and then again during the lives of the youngest people on the planet."

175. Oreskes and Conway, *The Collapse of Western Civilization*, 36, "A key attribute of the period was that power did not reside in the hands of those who understood the climate system, but rather in political, economic, and social institutions that had a strong

lege/university indoctrinated young voters despise climate-change deniers. Clearly, conservatives struggle against progressive activism by wasting precious energies, for sooner or later they morph into liberalism, bowing to the inevitable for maintaining a political livelihood.[176] In the aristocracy's light, conservatives of every age see the light and acknowledge from the backseat of the liberal vehicle commitment to social and cultural engineering. Conservatives ride, only slower, behind the liberals according to the migratory order into the depths of the Western heart.

For now the fire and the fury of the political left improvise a future for the West as a hegemonic one-party state[177] with technocrats the decision-makers. Simultaneously conservatives dream of living in a stable past that generation upon generation dissolves into a spent force. For the right as much as the left, each fails at constructing a sure community that will outlast erratic winds of change. Both political fronts, paradoxically, father limitless incapacities for assembling guidelines that define on-the-edge Western civilization, unable expressly in the Postmodern age even to simulate a lasting solidity. Each political entity lacks the fecundity to raise a philosopher "king" with a clear vision of stable government. As the large partisan divisions crowd each other for political gain, progressives and conservatives live and die amidst agonies of choice that divide and subdivide this civilization on the brink without a clear perspective to a sustainable future; no ordinary mortal survives long enough to grasp the course of the moments and movements that unmake Westernism.[178]

Yet, to make this alternative Westernism happen, an anti-democratic and god-like aristocracy with Big Tech authority motivates the left/liberal/progressives into an unknown day. Dominant aristocratic powers with

---

interest in maintaining the use of fossil fuels."

176. Proser, *Savage Messiah*, 219, "Online character assassination, threats of violence, exposure of private information (doxing), and de-platforming were becoming powerful weapons on both sides of the progressive/conservative divide."

177. Applebaum, *Twilight of Democracy*, 22, "It is a mechanism for holding power, and it functions happily alongside many ideologies."

178. Mishra, *Bland Fanatics*, 14, "While democracy was being hollowed out in the West, mainstream politicians and columnists concealed its growing void by thumping their chests against its supposed foreign enemies—or cheerleading its supposed foreign friends."

Ferguson, *Doom*, 9, "Disaster management is made still more difficult by the fact that our political systems increasingly promote into leading roles individuals who seem especially oblivious to the challenges described in the preceding paragraphs: subprime forecasters rather than superforecasters."

overwhelming authorities of wealth execute unregulated monopoly influences on governments of the West to shape legislation for progressive goals, thereto forming agreeable public opinions. When moneys of social platforms rival state and provincial economies, if not also Western countries, they impose with political ruthlessness the progressive will that destroys freedom of association. For the aristocracy through its Big Tech platforms harnesses the West to prosper progressive ideals in order to have this civilization succumb to another dimension without referendum consent; any imposition of soft totalitarianism initially defrauds Bottom-Tier individuals of liberty at the polls, never exciting storms of protest.

Governments of, by, and for the people provide times of inertia, when all collectively take and hold a deep breath. At each election call that breath explodes; conservatives and liberals then hasten to interpret the aristocrats' directives.

\/

Since 1945 a deep-reaching and far-ranging political initiative, leftism, encroached upon universities and colleges. Now the most intolerant Western educational institutions align with corporate human resource departments. Post-secondary schools indoctrinate at unbearable costs susceptible and sensitive students[179] in accommodation with left-wing philosophies; teachers prepare these persuadable young people for demonstrations in the streets, loud speakers in public squares, and managers of human resource offices that hire only fully woke employees. At the same time, human resource managers weed out the politically incorrect, dissidents[180] at odds with this woke generation. By disparaging true and tried Western motives and mores of Renaissance>Enlightenment>Modernist worlds, an unorthodox generation presses this civilization into inscrutable tomorrows, possibly a collection of totalitarian one-party states. As these indoctrinated young men and women[181] transmigrate into political leaders, social authorities,

---

179. Proser, *Savage Messiah*, 53, " . . . Marxism-Leninism ideology is being pumped into the soft heads of at least three generations of American students without being challenged or counterbalanced by the basic values of Americanism, American patriotism." The same occurs in Northern Europe and Australasia.

180. Dreher, *Live Not By Lies*, 40, " . . . institutions are embedding within their systems ideological tests to weed out dissenters."

181. Proser, *Savage Messiah*, 154, "Of course, if they challenged the wisdom or motives involved, they were punished with lesser grades, possibly even banishment, forfeiting tens or hundreds of thousands of dollar paid toward a degree that was promised to

SELF-EXAMINATION

and human resource managers they set trends and make moods favorable to the aristocracy, controlling thereby the thinking and the feeling of mass movements.

Political and social incentives to establish the leftist hierarchical mindfulness of the day eviscerate freedom of speech, apparently in swirling Postmodern relativities a minor but necessary sacrifice to stop conservative/right-wing opponents. It seems that left-wing authorities with a parental angst find that students are easily hurt, minorities are always traumatized, and communities-of-color are constantly victimized; they require paternal/maternal arbiters to protect them from right-wing damages. This robs not only the weak and wayward of speaking freely. In old Russia the communist leadership abused the bourgeoisie opposition with thought control and beat the defenseless proletariat into submission by an assembly of social constructs, however preposterous.

Explanatory: slowly, persistently in the West the socialist trajectory persuades university/college educated men and women to live by socialist>communist constructs. In the midst of Postmodernism's relativizing and now decades of raucous political action between liberals and conservatives, many find the socialist promises of stability, equity,[182] peace, and quiet enthralling.[183] With the fatherly or motherly hand of government controlling the issues of life from birth to death, numerous Westerners sacrifice the freedoms of democracy for the restraints of socialism/communism. Uneducated in the basics of democratic fundamentals, they do not recognize the abuse of personal freedoms, the poverty of state-controlled economics, and the privations suffered in the *gulags*.

\/

---

provide them with the key to wealth for life."

182. Equity: 1) The demand that Western governments with unlimited powers distribute economic resources equally to all. 2) Giving Westerners what each needs to enjoy a full life. 3) Impartiality and fairness for all. Briefly, equity involves a redistribution of wealth and upgrading of minority groups with "power to the people" that allows equal standing with majority Westerners. In fact, equity is a communist social construct: from all according to ability, for each according to need.

183. Shapiro, *The Authoritarian Moment*, 34, "Liberals see themselves as compassionate, at root; they see themselves through the lens of kindness."

Unsatisfied with Modernist power structures and rejecting its quintessence, specifically rule of law equitably administered by legitimate authorities,[184] Postmodern masses will topple governments, as once statues, to deliver the major shift of the day for the twenty-first century. As the cyclical swings—the 1960s civil rights movement,[185] the 1970s feminism (women competing with men on men's terms),[186] and the 1990s environmentalist maneuverings—make radical concepts more acceptable,[187] so now Postmodernism by relativizing social values and legal standards seeks to resettle the ways of feeling, thinking, and living for generations to come, everyone in lockstep emitting similar feelings, thought patterns, and recognizable assumptions. Allegedly, this sameness shows care for traumatized minorities, victimized races, and unprotected women by the exercise the governmental powers of a yet unidentifiable dictatorship managed by politically leftist speech controls. Such controls qualify news broadcasting, socialist/communist formation of familial, educational, governmental, and legal institutions, TV programming,[188] festivities, holidays, music/singing, sport activities, as well as other cultural phenomena, everything polarizing for non-participants. Not the governing individual of Modernism, but social classes of the twenty-first century will revive the old passions of Soviet or Maoist totalitarianism to determine social democracy, whether postmodern Neo-Marxism or Marxism Lite.[189]

---

184. Boyd, *Canadian Law*, 342, natural law: "A theory that has its roots in Judeo-Christian conceptions of social life. This theory holds that law and morality must be synonymous."

185. Harari, *Homo Deus*, 308, "North America and Western Europe experienced growing social unrest as radical left-wing movements strove to undermine the liberal order."

186. Smith, *A Concise History of New Zealand*, 201, "The Women's Liberation Movement burst onto the scene in 1972, in protest against being sentenced to housework, which they saw as restrictive." 201–202, "Late twentieth-century feminism grew from the international civil rights movement and anti-Vietnam War protests, and drew in particular on American influences. Young, urban, educated baby boomers—anti-racist, anti-sexist and socialist—campaigned for peace, the environment, and revolution, including sex roles."

187. Fukuyama, *Identity*, 105, "The 1960s witnessed the emergence of a series of powerful new social movements across the world's developed liberal democracies."

188. Shapiro, *Primetime Propaganda*, 2, "For almost its entire existence, television has been gradually perverted by a select group of leftist individuals who have used its power to foster social change through cultural 'messaging.'"

189. Proser, *Savage Messiah*, 1.
Lindsell, *The New Paganism*, 130. "Behind Marxism lies the idea found in philosophy

Self-Examination

Until the inroads of Postmodernism, Western liberalism unambiguously waved the flag of individualism, the sovereignty of the individual's elemental power,[190] which constituted the basis of politics and, more foundational, the liveliness of law. This quintessence of the West now faces falling over the brink into mass movements as represented on the one hand by the Marxist-based Critical Race Theory,[191] on the other by one-party leftist states in which power movements individuals mean nothing. Or, the West slides into right-wing dictatorships as in Hungary and Poland, systems of government that under tyrants also enforce mass mentality and group activity.[192] Now the mists of tomorrow still cover terrible contours of that day,[193] but from the Postmodern staging the West transitions, quietly or cruelly, into unknowns, the shadows of which sap individual strengths and responsibilities.

\/

Over the decades since the Second World War governments choose to rule by soft totalitarianism. Liberal and conservative political regimes entice

---

and religion that all people are brothers and sisters caught up in economic, political, and social systems that organize them into categories of masters and servants."

Boyd, *Canadian Law*, 13, "Marx argued that the relationship between material circumstances and human beings is dialectical in form."

190. Proser, *Savage Messiah*, 152, "Rejection of individual sovereignty was really the end of the world as Jordan (Peterson) knew it. Because it was the foundation of all Western law; the entire canon of Western civilization would collapse if it was dismissed. But that was exactly what was happening."

McKibben, *Falter*, 91, per Ayn Rand, "Government is bad. Selfishness is good. Watch out for yourself. Solidarity is a trap. Taxes are theft. *You're not the boss of me.*"

191. Dreher, *Live Not by Lies*, xii, "Under the guise of 'diversity,' 'inclusivity,' 'equity,' and other egalitarian jargon, the Left creates powerful mechanisms for controlling thought and discourse and marginalizes dissenters as evil."

Shapiro, *The Authoritarian Moment*, 55, "According to CRT, every institution in America is rooted in white supremacy; every institution is 'structurally' or 'institutionally' racist."

192. Proser, *Savage Messiah*, 152, "You don't have ideas and thoughts, you have what you've been socially conditioned to believe, and the exchange of ideas is nothing but a power game that's between groups of people opposing each other for predominance on the world stage."

193. Dreher, *Live Not by Lies*, xi, "Elites and elite institutions are abandoning old-fashioned liberalism, based on defending the rights of the individual, and replacing it with a progressive creed that regards justice in terms of groups. It encourages people to identify with groups—ethnic, sexual, and otherwise—and to think of Good and Evil as a matter of power dynamics among the groups."

respective citizens to depend on socialist measures—pensions, medical insurances, unemployment benefits, promises of higher minimum wages, safe injection sites, methadone dependencies, emergency funds, multi-million bail outs, dental programs, subsidies; etc. Whenever and wherever money is involved the Western tendency is to look for and seek out government aid. Such dependencies make citizens look to governments to provide rather than maintain bases of self-sufficiency. In this respect Northern Europe has gone further in relying on government moneys to sustain daily living.[194]

Through taxation political powers persuade people to hesitate before attacking specific policies or trends; biting the hand that feeds has consequences. Canada is moving fast in this direction;[195] America too follows in this trending. Australasians take more pride in freedom from state control. The reassuring fatherly hand or the appealing motherly touch, to say nothing of Big Brother's scrutinizing eye, coax the numerous of the West to rely on government largesse rather than on independent provisioning. Socialistic measures have become like breathing in oxygen; only when the oxygen supply ceases does thinking automatically focus on (more) government aid.

Bottom Tier Energies[196]

Western tardiness in depreciating dirty energy and idleness in appreciating clean energy raises the stakes for and against these power sources. Some side with fossil fuel to retain control over goods and services by promoting the cheaper advantages of bitumen, coal, and natural gas. Others side with electricity because of clean as well as renewable qualities. Both, supporters of dirty energy and proponents of clean energy, market ecological benefits. Each claims friendship with the environment and promises decreasing

---

194. Greenspan, *The Age of Turbulence*, 281, "Most of Europe was enthralled with one or more of the various forms of socialism."

195. Manthorpe, *Claws of the Panda*, 6, "Canada as a whole is suffering from the imposition of the values of the CCP on this country's citizens and institutions. Corruption in all its forms now permeates many walks of life. Most of this is Canada's own fault. Canada has become a haven for laundered fortunes of CCP princelings and red aristocrats (a privileged class whose status springs from family ties to the leadership of the CCP)." 7, "Canada is not alone in having these experiences flow from contact with the CCP. Similar things are happening in the United States, Europe, and especially New Zealand and Australia."

196. Rogan, *The Arabs*, 369. In 1973 the Arabs' oil ministries weaponized this fossil fuel to counteract Israel and the West generally.

Self-Examination

environmental pollutions, even easing climate warming. Electricity's producers seek the upper hand through wind and solar efforts for gain on the bottom line and for approval of new customers. Westerners presently caught between the industrial giants will crush the one or the other, the winner influencing the passage over the brink into a for now unrecognizable civilization.

As oil, coal, and gas industries concentrate to minimize electricity's worth, the producers of electrical energies for everyday living advertise abundant clean and cheap energy to ensure home heating and transportation by car, train, plane, and boat. Tensions across the West mount. Green technologies develop resources to counter climate warming. Many others hesitate because of conversion costs: dirty fuel is cheaper.

Money, in the billions if not trillions of tax-payer dollars/euros, gridlocks progress in the renovation of clean energy and reduction in climate warming, to duplicate the luxurious ways of the gods and goddess. Western hedonism in its covetousness faces a crisis over the edge for the next invention of the West. Engaged citizens and vote-conscious governments break with the tardiness of resistance incrementally to legislate production of renewable energy, thereby gaining limited environmental benefits.

As green technologies develop rich resources of renewable power, ionized battery technology too, the environmental advantage gathers impetus; slowly customer demands for clean energy breaks out of the idleness of resistance to face the hard facts of global climate change. Because of the gods and goddesses' driving force, the covetousness of Western hedonism intensifies the crisis in the immediate future, energy-conscious consumers push vote-conscious governments to legislate for the productivity of renewable sources of power.

Electricity as the energy norm decreases per day usage of millions of barrels of crude and as many tons of coal, plus cessation of fracking. Clean energy also means less reliance on anti-Western states for dirty fuels.

Both entities fight for huge financial benefits. Even as the West quietly slides over or violently topples into an unsure abyss, all citizens chose sides to control the battles and benefit from the winner in the next brutally discouraging civilization.[197]

---

197. Harari, *Homo Deus*, 314, "New technologies kill old gods and give birth to new gods."

IN THE WEST VERTICALLY

Bottom Tier Pollution

Everyday Westerners pollute and contaminate this civilization deep down, high up, and far away. Befouling and spoiling the human environment,[198] evident in a thousand ways, belongs to the Occidental manner and meaning of life. Carelessly disposing household goods, excessively spreading agricultural fertilizers,[199] burning dirty fuels, junking worn-out vehicles, continuing manufacturing inefficiencies, to mention only the more visible and odorous, despoil this civilization. The people of the West directly or indirectly with toxins and poisons impact the environment for global warming and life-wasting fears.

Westernkind's noxious wastes and disastrously disposed pollutants sully marine milieus,[200] damage the atmosphere, ruin ecosystems, breakdown biodiversity, and hazard human health for generations to come. Garbage along the waysides of life and foolishly disposed medications add to pending disasters.

Arbitrary dumping of environmentally harmful materials by dysfunctional Westernkind—thrash, garbage, industrial run-off, phosphorus, sulfuric acid, chlorofluorocarbons, greenhouse gasses, pesticides,[201] exhaust fumes, acidification, methane, human waste; etc., seeps into the water, leaches into the soil, and permeates into the air to injure every life form.[202]

---

198. McKibben, *Falter*, 53, "What a large team of scientists in 2017 called a 'biological annihilation' is already well under way, with half the planet's individual animals lost over the last decades and billions of local populations of animals already lost."

199. Gillam, *White Waste*, 15, " . . . from small towns to large cities, people are alleging connections between disease and glyphosate-based Roundup and say they were intentionally led to trust in the safety of a product that was not truly safe."

McKibben, *Falter*, 47, " . . . the overfishing, and the dead zones at the mouths of all major rivers where fertilizers pour into the sea, and the gyres of plastic spinning slowly a thousand miles offshore—these are the smallest of our insults to the ocean."

200. Winchester, *Pacific*, 429, " . . . [an ocean] that is now wearily compelled to absorb all the excesses of the humans who live beside and around." On it, too.

201. Carson, *Silent Spring*, 24, "For the first time in the history of the world, every human being is now subjected to contact with dangerous chemicals. In less than two decades of their use, the synthetic pesticides have been so distributed throughout the animate and inanimate world that they occur virtually everywhere." 25, "What sets the new synthetic insecticides apart is their enormous biological potency. They have immense power not merely to poison but to enter into the most vital processes of the body and change them in sinister and often deadly ways."

202. McKibben, *Falter*, 14-15, " . . . an interconnected world . . . offers a certain kind of stability—everyone in every country can all hear what the scientists warning of

This civilizational-wide contamination accuses consciences first all intent on money-making, with too little or less care about soiling the environment in which neighbors live to die. Poisoned milieus smite people, animals, and plants[203] with cancerous malignancies and life threatening pandemics. Through contamination the West changes as section by section falls over the rim into other worlds of disasters.

Electrifying the West comes slowly. Stranded on political recalcitrance and suffering from national insolvency the people of this civilization only with difficulty face the demands of decarbonization and sequestration of pollutants. Until the full engagement of solar and wind powers, Westerners wander about amidst dirty fuels and indissoluble plastics.

Bottom Tier Preservation

Evidence of losing the present West generates calls for legislation to ease through variable zones of transition; loss of this civilization to climate warming, under too slowly decomposing plastics, by rising ocean levels, and among more extensive landfill sites raises concerns for clean air, potable water, remediation of contaminated soil, and harvesting carbon dioxide. Yet only poorly coordinated efforts prefigure civilizational self-extermination. With detached national governments on one seat of the teeter-totter and engaged pressure groups, lobbies, and voters on the other, politicians left and right attempt to please all concerned at the same time and solve little. Only in halting ways Western legislators help the environment by preserving ecosystems, saving animal species from extinction,[204]

---

impending climate change say—but it removes the defense of distance."

203. Gillam, *White Waste*, 154, " . . . aggressive use of glyphosate year after year on farm fields led to a rise in glyphosate-resistant weeds, spurring many farmers to add more and more of the herbicide, often alongside other chemicals to fight back." 189–190. "Thwarting ever-higher doses of the weed killer, they just kept on growing, sinking roots deep down into farm fields, stealing nutrients and moisture from corn, cotton, soy, or other crops a farmer might try to grow."

204. Thunberg, *No One Is Too Small To Make a Difference*, 7, "Nor does hardly anyone ever mention that we are in the midst of the sixth mass extinction, with about 200 species going extinct every single day."

Winchester, *Pacific*, 242–243, "And just as the panda and the blue whale have come to symbolize both the beauty and the impermanence of mammalian life; and just as the creatures as the Bluefin tuna, the Grand Banks codfish, the dodo, and the great auk, and the Japanese flowering cherry blossoms come to stand for the precious fragility of nature, the Barrier Reef has come to stand for the earth's delicate and finely balanced frailty."

and providing crowded human communities with the necessities of acceptable living standards. As visions of choking on greenhouse gases, starving from insufficient food sources, and gagging on dirty drinking water—prime epidemiological causes for death—penetrate into the Bottom Tier, too few consciences respond and fewer care to initiate action, the whole seemingly irremediable.

As left-wing lobbyists seek more anti-polluting policies and projects—with public monies to match—hardcore remnants of climate-change deniers still whitewash the sinister day of reckoning. Unwilling to suffer the birthing pains of a cleaner world many place hope in a devil's bargain: weaker anti-pollution standards and more business-friendly legislation. In fact, anti-environmentalists, declared and undeclared, at times as nasty as *Antifa* rioters, turn a blind eye/deaf ear to the cross-currents of contaminants and hedonism. Westerners on the whole minimize the creeping horrors of climate warming and pollution, preferring to image the West a self-adjusting and self-purging ecosystem, whatever the garbage thrown into the environment of oceans, lakes, and streams. From the right, spokespeople preferentially discredit scientists whose research underpins the facts of rising sea waters and melting glaciers. All in all, too few Westerners follow the science; they seem consciously unaware of harm to the physical milieus, plants, and human communities whether in urban or rural settings. Liberals however, pull conservatives along, much as a ship drags its anchor along a sandy bottom.

In sum now: Westerners' excessive carbon dioxides[205] for one contribute to climate warming. Westerners' fossil-fuel fumes ruin breathing spaces. Westerners' dangerous vapors damage permafrost hugely. Westerners' deforestation hurts other ecosystems. As a frontline of defense, popular hopelessness and political vacillation stop Westerners from recognizing the roads of contamination into a destroyed civilization. The roadways into civilizational ruin are plain:

- Sloth with recyclables and garbage processing.

Morgan, *Australia*, 50, "Several types of kangaroos, wallabies, and emus were extinct by 1900."

Harari, *Homo Deus*, 33, "With regard to other animals, humans have long since become gods. We don't like to reflect on this too deeply, because we have not been particularly just and merciful gods."

205. McKibben, *Falter*, 21, "The molecular structure of carbon dioxide traps heat that would otherwise have radiated back to space."

- Minor care for degrading ecosystems and for worse-than-predicted breakdown of human communities.
- Weak support for legislation that builds a sustainable West.
- Strong fear factors that misunderstand dark complexities connected with climate change.
- Unwillingness to moderate immoderate lifestyles.
- Divided individualism for overcoming meteorological disasters.
- Waiting for governments to initiate remedial disaster repairs.
- Resistance to finish off crippling pandemonia.[206]
- Minds closed to civilization's massive slide into doomsday settings.

Even as environmentalists together encourage joint action during sweltering heatwaves,[207] monster storms, drowning floods, and destructive droughts they elevate Western failings at innovatively preventive solutions.

Bottom Tier Sundays

Sundays conform to the Western soul, overpowering all with sports, laying about, laziness, laying about, employment, laying about, gardening, laying about, seasonal activities, laying about, visiting, laying about, cottaging, laying about, partying, laying about, barbecuing, laying about, travelling, laying about, fundraising, laying about—for this is the weekend. As the last day of each week, Westerners define the Sunday in the Western way.

Bottom Tier Monarchy

British, Dutch, Belgian, Luxembourgian, Danish, Swedish, Norwegian, and Spanish monarchies with similar institutions in Andover, Lichtenstein, and Monaco, through serving heads of state grant respective countries stability in contrast to post-colonial republicanism. Republicanism with its volatile shifts in values mirrors the will of, by, and for the people.

---

206. Ferguson, *Civilization*, 17, " . . . Western elites are beset by almost millenarian fears of a coming environmental collapse."

207. McKibben, *Falter*, 59, "Sheer heat—heat alone, the most obvious effect of climate change—has begun to narrow the margins of our inhabitation. Nine of the ten deadliest heatwaves in human history have happened since 2000."

In the West Vertically

Under constitutional monarchies governments owe allegiance first to a king or queen, the present steadiness evident in Australia, Bahamas, Belize, Canada, Grenada, Solomon Islands, and New Zealand; in these countries Governor-Generals with penultimate authority represent the monarchy and approve parliamentary legislation. Governor-Generals also serve as Commanders-in-Chief, in which office to commit to the monarchial will. Only revolutionaries have republican plans.

As the West in this post-colonial era reflects republican or more likely socialist values, monarchy retains less of its steadying glories. Nevertheless when respective kings and/or queens speak, subjects take note and listen. As the monarchial identity in the West opposes the republicanism and socialism of former subject states, even dictatorships, the conflictive contrast draws a line through Western civilization.

Bottom Tier Agriculture

As Westerners' conspicuous consumption eats away at food sources and draws in hungry migrants from far-away places, this civilization courts disaster in the collective belly. Present abundances[208] wasted through uneaten foods thrown away by restaurateurs, unsaleable fruits/vegetables dumped by farmers on landfill sites, or left to spoil in the back of refrigerators by careless cooks (totaling as much as an estimated $40 billion annually) indicate unaffordable recklessness. Rotting foodstuffs speak of arrogance at the center of luxury with warnings of the hubris that reinvents the West.

1–4. Hungry school children, undernourished elders, and derelict homeless shame the well-to-do along with vote-conscious city fathers and mothers. Needs in the West to carry sufficing consumption patterns down into the various levels of the lower Bottom-Tier dwellers to feed the actually famished hammer away on walls of covetousness, for upper-class greediness leaves the malnourished with less. And less. While middle-class residents, the bourgeoisie, at home in the shades of the Top Tier polishing away mouthwatering delicacies may care little, or less, for all low on the food chain, the actually hungry rely on soup kitchens and handouts for sustenance, with *dining experiences* on hotdogs and potato chips. While those high up in the Bottom Tier may for the length of a dining experience ingest

---

208. Harari, *Homo Deus*, 55, "Thanks to artificial fertilisers, industrial insecticides and genetically modified crops, agricultural production nowadays outstrips the highest expectations ancient farmers had of their gods."

an approximation of social climbing into the Top Tier, many proletarians daily feel the reality of hunger. At the very bottom the poorest of the poor live out of the goodness of soup kitchens, school children subsist on meal programs five days per week throughout the school year, and the invisible elderly poor eat out of after best-before cans. To say it plainly, consumption patterns in the West leave the marginalized expendable along with food/water refugees struggling for better food and cleaner water, while the richer fight ineffectively with dietary regimes.

2–4. As cities swell and industrial parks grow—along with land-swallowing four-lanes to prevent traffic congestion—agricultural lands, always a limited resource, fade away under building foundations and bitumen-black roadbeds; loss of carelessly abused prime farmlands entails more costly imports from foreign sources to satisfy today's food lusts, the freight costs and pollution impacts thereof mocking hungry school children, penny-pinching seniors, and the destitute wandering between soup kitchens. Covering dairy and crop lands with asphalt depletes meat, grain, and milk production to leave in an era of climate change also the Western population victim to floods and droughts, storms and heatwaves that hurt most directly expendable human beings, often enough the careworn on lowest societal rungs barely able to find simplest necessities, or go without. Incidentally, wasting agricultural lands runs the West onto the cusp of disaster, the aftermath of which unprecedented woe with malnourishment.

3–4. Genetic engineering, large-scale farming, wasteful fertilizer applications, along with huge importing industries may provide for all higher and highest on the West's societal rungs. Sustainability, however, at nourishing the billions in the long run means that eventually only the moneyed may purchase food at inflated prices, leaving others struggling on depleted soils, over sagging water tables, and in harrowing food deserts. The wealthy then patronize well-stocked grocery stores, indulge in high-end eating experiences, and live comfortably far above the poverty line while exposing exporting countries to contemporary methods of re-colonization.

4–4. Elimination of large-scale farming and huge herds of cattle may along with vegetarianism and veganism offset imbalances in food resources, temporarily; the rule of numbers throughout Western populations pose brooding feuds, the have-not envious of the haves and the bourgeoisie wary of the *lumpenproletariat*.

In the West Vertically

Trifling with Western agricultural resources makes crop failures and food shortages worse, never mind how much speculators rely on grain and pork-belly futures.

Bottom Tier Employment

In the West employment depends on money, even among climate-change deniers. The time-is-money mentality dominates in boardroom decisions, CEO forecasts, and employees' wages—no money, no work. Hence, even the overstated axiom—work hard, play by the rules[209]—pays off supposedly also for menial laboring. Money controls promotions, job searches, and retirement benefits. Money is the West's lifeblood, the first part of the duopoly in every place of employment; the other part involves working conditions. Whatever concomitant economic stresses, recession or inflation, the brutal functioning of money governs employment situations. This money and incessantly working for money declares who you are: working to live rather than living to work. Working to live gives numerous many the meaning of life, thus handicapping desires to be industrious.

This civilization's fragile boom-and-bust economy follows the invisible hand of the free market,[210] even though in the market place capitalism still preferable to socialism's soft tyranny and slow slide into communism.[211] As

---

209. Hedges, *America,* 30, "The heady dreams and promises of youth in postindustrial America have shattered. The mantra, preached by the coach, of hard work, team-work, a positive attitude, and the mythical values of America has been exposed as a fraud."

Steyn, *Lights Out,* 176, "The obvious defect in Communism is that it's decrepit and joyless and therefore of limited appeal."

210. Hedges, *America,* 5, "[Marx] knew that reigning ideologies—think corporate capitalism with its belief in deindustrialization, deregulation, privatization, austerity, slashing of social service programs, and huge reductions in government spending—were created to serve the interests of the economic elites, since 'the class which has the means of material production at its disposal, had control at the same time over the means of mental production.'" See: Karl Marx, *The German Ideology,* New York: International Publishers, 1970, 64.

Thatcher, *The Downing Street Years,* 11, "... a vast sensitive nervous system, responding to events and signals all over the world to meet the ever-changing needs of the peoples in different countries, from different classes, of different religions, with a kind of benign indifference to their status."

211. Ferguson, *Civilization,* 207, "The founders of communism, Karl Marx and Friedrich Engels, were just two of many radical critics of the industrial society, but it was their achievement to devise the first internally consistent blueprint for an alternative social order. Since this was the beginning of a schism within Western civilization that

SELF-EXAMINATION

Australasia, Northern Europe, and North America stumble from bear market to bull market, the people low in the Bottom Tier orient living around soup kitchens and food banks. Business powers since the Second World War outsourced industries that provided affordable housing, well-paid jobs, properly funded schools, dependable public transit, community-oriented police forces, affordable health care—all in all, the strengths of middle class living.[212] Now factory hulks and empty warehouses dominate city skylines in run-down areas and employment seekers spent endless hours on-line or in-line, too many for the few opportunities available. The drudgery, monotony, and slavishness by waiting in lines apparently are better than manual labor and struggling for subsistence. Apparently also, the wheels of consumerism, despite its periodic recoveries, fail to turn the economic wheels efficiently.[213]

In this boom-or-bust context, robotics sends shivering anticipation or trembling fear through workplaces and job seekers; for AI technology changes the West.[214] Powers of computation and automation—unstoppable by Luddites—set parameters for the economy of coming decades; these remove the barriers of time and remuneration. With digital work and commerce keys to entrepreneurial inventiveness and prosperity, the stakes are high. Those who cannot keep up drift down to the bottom-most level of the Bottom Tier, to languish there in the proximity of handouts. All who can compete emerge as winners. As the working gap between human beings and machines shrinks, artificial intelligence shows ways ahead that temporarily make the West hesitate on the edge before confronting new hazards.

---

would last for nearly a century and a half, it is worth pausing to consider the origins of their theory."

Fukuyama, *Identity*, 7, "A long tradition dating back at least as far as Karl Marx sees political struggles as a reflection of economic conflicts, essential as fight over shares of the pie."

212. Toynbee, *Civilization On Trial*, 21, "The future of the Western middle class is in question now in all Western countries; but the outcome is not simply the concern of the small fraction of mankind directly affected; for this Western middle class—this tiny minority—is the leaven that in recent times has leavened the lump and has thereby created the modern world."

213. Contrarian: Marsden, *The Twilight of the American Enlightenment*, 12, "Consumerism had become a nearly all-controlling force in the modern era."

214. Harari, *Homo Deus*, 53, "... once technology enables us to re-engineer human minds, Homo sapiens will disappear, human history will come to an end and a completely new kind of process will begin, which people like you and me cannot comprehend."

At other times pains of employee shortages hinder production schedules as well as contractual commitments; governments stimulate immigration and entice seasonal workers with interesting pay schedules to solve arbitrary problems.[215]

Bottom Tier Volunteering

In Western society many find themselves morally compelled to give back to the community benefits earned through employment. Such volunteering may be interpreted in many ways—prime targets: assisting elementary school teachers with slow learners, easing the workload of hospital staff, helping minor league sports beginners with the basics, taking part in civic committees to resolve local issues, sorting and packaging in food banks, picking up garbage, critiquing a manuscript, providing an endorsement/reference, collecting money through a walkathon/bikeathon, or helping an elderly person through a busy intersection. Driven by guilt, many move about in community settings to give back.

Many too with the milk of human kindness or perhaps to escape the isolation of loneliness,[216] seek social contacts, thereto willingly and effortlessly reshuffling schedules to benefit others and thereby making societal openness attractive. Still others need to top-up deflating self-esteem and find volunteering necessary to earn points for self-righteousness, therewith to please the gods and goddesses.

Whatever its meat and bone, volunteering in its numerous interests makes participants feel good about themselves and worthy of the deities' blessings.

Bottom Tier Legality

Progressives find common law developed over centuries by trial and error inadequate for Modernism>Postmodernism. While conservatives prize literal, natural interpretations of founding documents and the common laws

---

215. Fukuyama, *Identity*, 6, "Anti-immigrant and anti-EU parties gained strength in many other developed countries, most notably the National Front in France, the Party for Freedom in the Netherlands, the Alter-native for Germany, and the Freedom Party in Austria."

216. McKibben, *Falter*, 113, "All told, loneliness is as bad for you physically as obesity and smoking."

SELF-EXAMINATION

based on these crucial fundamentals,[217] liberals mistrust and distrust the governing intentions of the 1215 British *Magna Carta*, the 1787 American *Declaration of Independence*, the 1867 *British North American Act*, which became the Canadian 1982 *Constitution Act*, the 1900 Australian *Constitution Act*,[218] the 1840 New Zealand *Treaty of Waitangi*,[219] the 1972 *European Communities Act*, and many older Northern European founding documents to regiment the rule of law.[220] Alternatively, with a set of assumptions opened up by rights-based manifestoes, the progressives facilitate social engineering to make the West a superior world, thereby cleverly solidifying extremes in selfishness.[221] With the flexibilities of human rights progressives unseat conservative restraints to declare this civilization the laboratory for glorifying its visceral slide into more of wokeism's toughness.

Interpreters of the more prominent human rights invention, the 1948 *Universal Declaration of Human Rights*, [222] mobilize waves of feminism,

---

217. Boyd, *Canadian Law*, 5, "Law is a vitally important force; it is the skeleton that structures our economic, social, and political lives."

218. Morgan, *Australia*, 21, "When the Commonwealth of Australia was inaugurated in 1901, the new nation was a white bastion in the Pacific."

219. Smith, *A Concise History of New Zealand*, 47, "Struggles for land have swirled around the Treaty of Waitangi of 6 February 1840, and instrument unique less in its making than in what it has become—for indigenous rights and as a mission statement for a single country—with grand goals achieved at minimal coast."

220. Ferguson, *The Great Degeneration*, 15, " . . . like the English common law, the rules evolve organically, as judges weigh up the competing claims of precedent and the changing needs of society."

221. Predilection for self-centeredness happens through carrying watches and wearing fitness socks that monitor blood oxygen levels, track sleep patterns, sort through exercise exertions, log water intake, measure heart beats, calculate stress levels, chart caloric burnings, keep up with cadence movements, open foot-landing techniques to inspection, treasure fun competitions, and much more, which monitoring consumes total interest in the self.

Branden, Nathanial, "Isn't Everyone Selfish?" in Rand, *The Virtue of Selfishness*, 58, "A genuinely selfish man knows that only reason can determine what is, in fact, to his self-interest, that to pursue contradictions or attempt to act in defiance of the facts of reality is self-destructive—and self-destruction is not to his self-interest."

Fukuyama, *Identity*, 12, "Modern economics is based on one such theory, which is that human beings are 'rational utility maximizers': they are individuals who use their formidable cognitive abilities to benefit their self-interest."

222. Fukuyama, *Identity*, 137–138, "The 1947 Universal Declaration of Human Rights became the basis for a growing body in international law that asserted that rights are inherent in all human beings and need to be respected by all nations."

hardline racial equity, virulent anti-sexism;[223] etc. By banking on another authoritarianism, a soft tyranny,[224] thereby imposes upon the West implacable rules of mastery concerning women's health,[225] euthanasia, and anti-discrimination in places of employment. Through legislated social and cultural engineering, progressives plan to remake Western civilization by adulterating basic legal systems with modifications that ignore individual responsibility and accountability, thus turning (national) governments into father-figures and/or mother-figures manipulating dependent citizens with cradle-to-grave entitlements.

Champions of human rights insert these legal structures on all levels—international, national, provincial/state, and civic—to facilitate Western society's liberal state of mind; with stubborn resolve they recast the West into another utopia. Thereby they on the left integrate George Orwell's *1984* and Aldous Huxley's *Brave New World* into the main stream of life, however selfish and tyrannical the governments that eventually evolve. Human rights activists little consider the consequences of building a progressive utopia[226] and neighbor love even less; they self-identify as the creators of a portentous world governed equitably per identity politics, its logic based on and decided by quasi-sciences of the day.[227] Increased impersonalization, forestalled trust in governments, loss of respect for police forces, and an ambiguous reliance on court systems further corrupt the liberal social hopes and racial dynamics; human rights legalities pull and push Western citizens into the lows of covetousness: *my* rights excite personal authoritarianism for control. With rights legislation Westerners became litigious people, ready to sue and countersue to exact financial benefits from a mistake, an error in judgment, or a past legislative program now considered erroneous.

To achieve tyrannical control over the West more Westerners in the socialist>communist manner take to the streets, protesting established

---

223. Streissguth, *Hate Crimes*, 143, sexism: "The view that holds one sex to be superior to the other, either in intellectual or physical capacity."

224. Applebaum, *Twilight of Democracy*, 25, " . . . it relies upon a cadre of elites to run the bureaucracy, the state media, the courts, and, in some places, state companies."

225. Women's health: euphemistically covering government-sponsored release of abortifacients and government-paid killing of unborn children.

226. Packer and Howard, *Christianity*, 25, "Humanism, like Marxism, sees itself as pointing the way to an ideal society. It is, in other words, a form of utopianism."

227. Lindsell, *The New Paganism*, 190, "[Scientism] is designed to advance empiricism to an absolute that denies the supernatural and thus becomes at best irrational."

SELF-EXAMINATION

laws, always conscious of aristocratic aims; marchers enforce human rights riotously, break legislation undemocratically, and influence court decisions calamitously.²²⁸ In wild protestations the minions of progressive leaders, often burning and looting, generate support for more revolutionary human rights, hence wokeism.²²⁹

\/

As Western progressives improvise a world-ideal community, a total utopia, Postmodernism rolls a wet blanket over envisioned specifics, disrupting this society of the future. With distrust of government, loss of respect for police forces, and ambiguous reliance on court decisions leftist methodologies pollute this progressive eternity of blessedness. Without a sure foundations wokeist utopianism constantly fails.

Nevertheless, with Postmodern dynamics of relativizing social and cultural engineering, woke proponents move the West over the precarious precipice into worse conglomerations of dictatorial societies, now its basic means shaming contrarian voices into silence and submission. Until the day over the brink, progressives find the courts of public opinion most useful and therefore most deleterious to the Western baseline grounded in reason, science, languages, and, above all, the Renaissance>Enlightenment>Modernist expression of individualized freedom.²³⁰ Wokeism pushes and pulls more Westerners down the migratory order into the West's inner ugliness, ultimate darkness, never ever to see a sunrise.

---

228. Hedges, *America*, 270, "The militant believes it is only in the streets and in acts of civil disobedience that change is possible."

229. Shapiro, *The Authoritarian Moment*, 80, "Wokeism . . . is rooted in identity politics. It takes cues from intersectionality, which suggests a hierarchy of victimhood in which you are granted credibility based on the number of victim groups to which you belong. But it doesn't stop there. Wokeism takes identity politics to the ultimate extreme; it sees *every structure of society* as reflective of deeper, underlying structures of oppression."

Fukuyama, *Identity*, 9–10, "Identity grows, in the first place, out of a distinction between one's true inner self and an outer world of social rules and norms that does not adequately recognize that inner self's worth or dignity."

This worth of the inner self reflects current Gnosticism.

230. Shapiro, *The Authoritarian Moment*, 88, "Where Enlightenment liberalism had taken for granted certain ideas about human rights, the value of objective truth, and the ability for human beings to understand the world around them—ideas borrowed from Judeo-Christianity—and then built on those ideas by questioning long-held but unproven axioms about science and power, deconstructionism bathed *everything* in the acid of questioning, hence 'deconstructing' everything."

As tyrannous anti-authoritarianism[231] breaks down remnants of Modernism for the final defeat of Renaissance logic, this other way of determining right from wrong creeps into Western minds and hearts to make critical qualifiers change; wokeist moral conduct now depends on the momentary preferences of identity politics and transitory agreements with authority structures that hinge on equity inclinations. In the long run, because of Postmodernism, the West's legal narrative suffers the loss of neighbor love, identity politics the philosophical/ethical default.[232] As progressives reshape Western civilization, left-wing *Antifa* rioters inflexibly break open antipathies to come.

Wokeism[233] from inception in its Postmodern bedding became an enormous multi-lane round-about with multiple entry ramps. This round-about draws in the racialized and benighted peoples, all answering to the summons to remake the Western world into a distortion of the present civilization. In its enlarging to accommodate more hitherto ill-treated tribes, this round-about eventually too drops over the edge to deliver its people in another, more tyrannous world.

Bottom Tier Anti-Semitism

Even though reactions to the 1939–1945 Holocaust curbed hatred against the Jews and the 1947 formation of the State of Israel disarmed measures of guilt for tolerating this Nazi brutality, anti-Semitism metastasized throughout the West, right-wing extremists spouting insults at Jews and left-wing radicals supporting Palestinian aggression as well as financing Hamas' hostility at obliterating Israel. The existence of the Jewish people as Israelis

---

231. Applebaum, *Twilight of Democracy*, 56, "Unity is an anomaly. Polarization is also normal. Skepticism about liberal democracy is also normal. The appeal of authoritarianism is eternal."
Shapiro, *The Authoritarian Moment*, 5, "Human beings are ripe for authoritarianism."

232. Thatcher, *The Downing Street Years*, 147, "Authority of all kinds—in the home, the school, the churches, the state—had been in decline for most of the post-war years."
Harpur, *God Help Us*, 39, "Private conduct, as long as no law is broken, becomes totally 'a law unto itself.'"

233. Fukuyama, *Identity*, 6, "'The left has focused less on broad economic equality and more on promoting the interests of a wide variety of groups perceived as being marginalized—blacks, immigrants, women, Hispanics, the LGBT community, refugees, and the like."
This explains the Biden/Harris presidency's open border between the USA and Mexico.

serves as a flashpoint of xenophobic outpourings of hatred that involve the West repeatedly at resolving polarizations of racist violence.

Undying anti-Semitism arouses irreconcilable hostilities, which under twentieth-century Nazism/Hitlerism reached a temporary zenith and maliciously blighted Western civilization. Still the hatred continues, low-key perhaps, on social media, the Jews accused of all sorts of vices, the worst that they control everything. Anti-Semitism as an open sewer with many branches runs through the West, each flooded with the Jewish Question,[234] the answer to which flows with this civilization over the brink into worse cascades of restrictive hatreds.

Bottom Tier Xenophobia

In the West from the right and from the left boiling animosities collide. They in the middle, the large majority, hope against hope to escape the bruising impacts, except from respective recliners and couches to watch the self-consuming mayhem unfold on social media. White supremacist spirits[235] out of resurgent nationalism and Brown anti-racists out of visionary internationalism—each with rank crudities of racial discrimination intend on dominating the end flow of this civilization's history.[236] Proudly, it is presumed, Caucasians represent the pinnacle of the human race and claim attribution for all mechanical/technological advancements over the last centuries. Antithetically, with anticipation, it is assumed, nascent minority races will in the twenty-first century own the West, to the victors the spoils.[237] Meanwhile, xenophobia reigns.

Caucasians have powerful worries that the political left will sell the West for votes to other races, thus to maintain the aristocracy's divine interests in continuity. Paleo-conservative groupings alive with xenophobia,

---

234. Tenold, *Everything You Love Will Burn*, 63, 225, 234.

235. Streissguth, *Hate Crimes*, 143, white supremacist: "Someone who believes that white (European-descended) people should hold a dominant place over people of other ethnicities, such as black or Asian."

236. Mishra, *Bland Fanatics*, 8, "The suspicion that 'Islamo-fascism' had declared war on liberalism roused many Anglo-American intellectuals into a bolder attempt to make the world over again in their preferred image of Anglo-America."

237. Ferguson, *Civilization*, 177, "Racism was not some backward-looking reactionary ideology; the scientifically uneducated embraced it as enthusiastically as people today accept the theory of man-made global warming."

isolationism, too often misogyny, and even neo-Nazi ideals[238] rise up against the left and the left with social and cultural engineering and money will repress the whites into an endangered minority. To fight this left-wing engineering right-wingers reject the shambles of political correctness, exercising free speech to offend women and minorities. In the meantime, from the left hate groups as *Antifa*[239] with anti-Fascist determination roil against the right with accusations derived from Critical Race Theory, at every meeting point with the right breaking out its loathing with violence,[240] burning, looting, and anti-authoritarian hate.

Unbridgeable hatreds burn on the edges of the West and open flames consume this Aryan civilization to remake this world into images of the Left or the Right, and everyone so aligned heads down into more chaotic xenophobia.

Bottom Tier Justice

Beginning with the poorest of the lower Bottom-Tier classes, blacks and indigenous the predominantly incarcerated, the weight of the Western judicial system as a whole falls on the weaker, those who commit lesser crimes in comparison to fraud, grand theft, and treason found in higher social echelons. Many among the racialized in penitentiaries integrate measures of black pride[241] to survive. Outcries to reform justice and the judicial systems turn into whispers of hopelessness the closer this civilization approaches in the fast passage of time to the precipice of no return, after which the abused the abusers.

---

238. Streissguth, *Hate Crimes*, 141, Neo-Nazi: "An individual who subscribes to the beliefs and practices of Adolf Hitler and Nazi Germany."

239. Tenold, *Everything You Love Will Burn*, 190, "'Antifa' is a catchall term for a scattered movement of radical leftists, comprising people who reject nationalism and fascism on a visceral level."

Hedges, *America*, 195, "Antifa and the black bloc oppose organized movements. This ensures their powerlessness. They call for preemptive violence—what adherents call 'collective self-defense'—and insist that those whom they, and they alone, define as 'fascists' deserve to be violently attacked and silenced."

240. Streissguth, *Hates Crimes*, 3, "Since antiquity, humans have been selecting other humans for assault, injury, and murder for their different appearance, color, nationality, language, or religion."

241. Tenold, *Everything You Love Will Burn*, 230, "There was a need for black power and pride because the African American community had been disempowered, disenfranchised and shackled—figuratively and literally—for generations."

Self-Examination

Bottom Tier Medicine

Relative to medicine and surgery, veterinarians, Western pharmacists, and physicians repeatedly recalibrate skills in healing. In this respect the West outshines African, East Asian, South American, and indigenous therapeutic healers[242] to recreate soundness in minds and bodies. The efficacies of North American, Northern European, and Australasian healing services learned on battle fields and in hospitals save human lives by following science-based methodologies. Much the same applies to veterinarian services for all sorts of animals, an aspect of stewardship caring, somewhat less endearing than healing hurting people.[243]

The efficacy of Western medicine applies specifically now to fighting infectious diseases, in the twentieth century the Spanish flu and in the twenty-first century the contagious and unpredictable novel coronavirus dubbed Covid-19 or SARS-CoV-2.[244] In the 2019–2022 pandemic with its variants, the Delta in particular, governments through social restrictions and pharmaceuticals by way of vaccines and injection procedures took control also over its other deadly mutations. At the same time governments seek to still anxieties aggravated by lockdowns, unemployment,[245] and shuttered businesses, on-line education, and long socially isolated citizens.

Slowly, through Western-created vaccines and vaccination procedures the novel coronavirus came to heel, its mutants also submissive to contemporary medicinal ingenuity. Undoubtedly the social transformations governments legislated helped win the fight against this epidemic and spurred

---

242. In such research indigenous healers seek to understand human relationships to the natural world in order to bring about wider reconciliation within respective Western communities; the natural world establishes a common bond.

243. Harpur, *God Help Us*, 19, "There must be compassion and respect for every living creature and for the Earth itself."

244. Mishra, *Bland Fanatics*, 13, "The coronavirus cruelly exposed the reality that [British and American exceptionalism] had long concealed: heavily indebted states, bailed-out corporations, impoverished working classes, and eviscerated public health systems." 14, "What has becomes clearer since the coronavirus crisis is that modern democracies have for decades been lurching towards moral and ideological bankruptcy—unprepared by their own publicists to cope with the political and environmental disasters that unregulated capitalism inflicts, even on such winners of history as Britain and the US."

Ferguson, *Doom*, 119, "The history of disease is a protracted interaction between evolving pathogens, insect or animals carriers, and human social networks."

245. Saul, *The Unconscious Civilization*, 14, " . . . the marketplace these days is into job elimination."

faith in the aristocracy, its humanism and humanitarianism tenaciously powerful.

Across the West warding off the inevitability of death for people, first for the rich and then also for the poor, along with animals, highly-trained healers spread across the broad spectrum of life, delivering:

- Ingenuity in medical and surgical methodologies to preserve human life.[246]
- Veterinarian advances to save animals large and small.
- Hospitalization to optimize healing.

On various levels and from different sources Westerners encourage the flow of life, healing minds and bodies. Losing this pharmaceutical and medical fidelity and ingenuity to the savagery of quacks looms tragically.

Bottom Tier Death

To escalate the worth of the deceased, Westerners in public and private memorials celebrate life with protocols that pretend that death is a normal element of existence. Therefore Westerners, typically ingenuous at manufacturing wealth, invented social mechanisms that for a price deny the radicality of dying. Different sorts of end-of-life procedures dampen pains of bereavement, except for suicides.

- Cremation/incineration to declare with finality the end of a human life, eliminating existence beyond the present.[247]
- Euthanasia to evade experiencing and/or seeing physical as well as mental/emotional suffering of a slow death.
- Abortion to regulate family planning and women's health by *painlessly* removing the results of conception, the same also for sex-selection procedures.

---

246. Ferguson, *Civilization*, 145, "The timing of the 'health transition'—the beginning of sustained improvements in life expectancy—is quite clear. In Western Europe it came between the 1770s and the 1890s, beginning first in Denmark, with Spain bringing up the rear."

247. Bonhoeffer, tr. Eberhard Bethge, *Ethics*, 107, "Slow pain is more feared than death."

- Eugenics to improve the constituency of race, to cleanse the human gene pool from inferior peoples.[248]

In the context of Western eugenics, tinkering with DNAC surgically clears out genetic illnesses and deformities into enhancements of the human race, one fetus at a time.

- Suicide to escape accountability for social conflict and/or defeat in moral striving burdens only relatives with extremes of guilt.
- Killing by the entertainment industry to generate suspense and/or terminate a plot in a satisfying manner.

In the permissive mind of the West death removes problem situations, eases weights resting on relatives, and allows in many circumstances celebration of lives lived.[249] Now the will to live degenerates into its opposite.

In the West life is cheap, a meanness aggravated by its gun-culture. Manufactures of guns, employers of mules, and sellers of guns alike according to artificial self-esteem, typically Western, are not bad people; many are men and women seeking to get by and provide for respective families. Weapons, especially assault types, on the black market are simply toys. Only, rashes of violence in homes and on streets leave the dead behind and relatives in passive sorrow, both proving that individual worth counts for little, if not less. Drug cartels and street gangs make war zones in which to operate with impunity, money-wise underworlds that thrive in the West.

---

248. Ferguson, *Civilization*, 177, "Here was the ultimate solution to the problem of public health: a master-race of superhumans, bred to withstand the attacks of pathogens."

McKibben, *Falter,* quoting one Marcy Darnovsky, 148, "Allowing any form of human germline modification leaves the way open for all kinds—especially when fertility clinics start offering genetic upgrades to those able to afford them."

249. Packer and Howard, *Christianity*, 21–22, "The notorious willingness of some humanists to justify and recommend abortion, infanticide, euthanasia, and the sterilizing or killing of the physically handicapped and mentally limited, as the Nazis did, is clear evidence of the direction in which their basic attitude takes them."

Shapiro, *The Authoritarian Moment*, 49, "Margaret Sanger, founder of Planned Parenthood, called for the sterilization or quarantining of some 'fifteen or twenty millions of our populations' in order to prevent the supposed poisoning of the gene pool."

IN THE WEST VERTICALLY

Bottom Tier Dissent

Current public protests and street riots,[250] hallmarks of socialism>communism, activate more Bottom-Tier Westerners in reaction to critical events, police brutality,[251] judicial decisions, and unpopular laws. Such reflexive woke demonstrations inflame courts of public opinion as well as social structures throughout Western civilization.

By minimizing or deriding processes of rational discourse and evading ballot box proceedings to register disagreement and/or influence legislative decisions, protesters and rioters now regularly and intentionally alter Western culture, in the process toppling statues, altering street names, renaming public buildings, rebranding sport franchises, and revising history, of the latter the 1619 movement an example. As aborigines, immigrants, and refugees (minority groupings) gain a voice they remake Western civilization to shape a meta-narrative in which they mirror themselves, the whole entirely subjective.

- North American aborigines move with tribal unity based on a mythical Turtle-Island origination for the survival of life on this planet.
- Racial minorities through identity politics seek liberated statuses as power assertions within host countries.
- Protestations, peaceful or with burning violence, implant from the top down the organizers' plans for a non-Caucasian West.

Dissension has the downfall of the West at heart, preparation for an insufferable over-the-edge future.

Bottom Tier Transportation

The West lives by mobility for the freedom of movement that contributes to the dominance of this civilization; cars, trucks, airplanes, trains, and boats

---

250. Hedges, *America*, 191, "Marching as an anonymous mass—in black with faces covered—overcomes alienation, feelings of inadequacy, powerlessness, and loneliness. It provides comradeship. It allows an inchoate rage to be unleashed on any target." 199, "Street clashes do not distress the ruling elites. These clashes divide the underclass. They divert activists from turning on structures of power. They give the corporate state the justification to impose harsher forms of control and expand the powers of police."

251. Hedges, *America*, 265, "Police function as predators in impoverished communities."

serve for transporting peoples and goods, everything too much for the survival of this civilization.

On land the building of roads removes traffic congestions by destroying agricultural lands and aquafers with fatal results for food production.

Everywhere the greenhouse gassing of the West imperils populations on every continent.

Western inventiveness may depress carbon dioxide poisoning by electrifying every country. Westerners' demands for right of way in matters of transportation carries this civilization over speed bumps into more lawless traffic congestions.

Bottom Tier Communication[252]

From telegramming, radio, telephone, and television to computerization,[253] Western information moves at awesome speeds. In the difference between the rapidity of smoke signals, semaphores, the pony express, telegraph, telephone, and nanosecond messaging, the Occidental speed of data movements excites entrepreneurs to discover ever faster ways of communication.[254]

Shooting past attention deficits and information overloads, Internet managers (threaten to) censor racially and sexually explicit posts, fake news, rank crudities of death threats, and fight hacking attacks that interfere with leftist scheming to re-morph the West with instant communication.[255]

---

252. Proser, *Savage Messiah*, 201, "There's a technological revolution, it's a deep one. The technological revolution is online video and audio immediately accessible to everyone all over the world. And so what that's done is . . . it's turned the spoken word into a tool that has the same reach as the printed word. So it's a Gutenberg revolution in the domain of video and audio and it might be even deeper than the original Gutenberg revolution because it isn't obvious how many people can read but lots of people can listen . . .. Now all of a sudden we have this forum for long-form discussion, real long-form discussion, and it turns out that everyone is way smarter than we thought, right? We can have these discussions publicly."

Harari, *Homo Deus*, 254, "As the Communist Manifesto brilliantly put it, the modern world positively requires uncertainty and disturbance."

253. Winchester, *Pacific*, 103–104, " . . . slowly, beating against the undertow of traditional thinking . . . and through the mist the vision of the true Japanese transistor started to solidify."

254. Winchester, *Pacific*, 110, "The term consumer electronics was instantly coined to describe this new business—backed by an industry that was born on the Pacific Rim, and has in one form or another come to play a sustaining central role in the betterment of human life, in most corners of the world."

255. Ferguson, *Doom*, 11, "The advent of the internet has greatly magnified the

In the West VERTICALLY

The excitements of data delivery diminish the worthiness of once vibrant social institutions—libraries, lodges, civic committees, clubs, and associations—as well as churches to prevent many necessary conversations; for social media on current platforms never resolve the isolation of individualism, much less the social divide imposed by the identity politics.[256] The eroding values of many traditions and bodies contribute to the loneliness and brokenness taking shape over the rim for victims of left-wing ideation.

Despite god-like tech giants' boast that the Internet's instant communication unites the world community, specifically now Western homogeneity, actually Westerners rancorously divide and subdivide. Individualist Westerners shaped by Modernism and confused by Postmodernism arrange and rearrange beyond multicultural groupings into temporary clusters of interest. By and large, they rally around old-age left/right, black/white, east/west, and north/south rifts. Algorithms in effect segregate the dynamics of society into wild-west Internet revolutions monitored by left-wing censorship that restricts freedom of speech, the whole from any current perspective ungovernable, except by raw power. The promise of the social networks to unify the West into a socialist utopia where all have the freedom to speak without restrictions bows to the public will; on the many platforms users prefer the boundaries of tribalism, hedonism, and subjectivism.

Now censorship happens. 1) Big Tech dominates in communication, empowering the managers of the platforms to remove whatever fails to conform to left-wing politics.[257] 2) These managers also shutdown servers in specific countries, the leaders of which fear the free flowing of information that threatens governmental survivability. Here are two ways of

---

potential for misinformation and disinformation to spread, to the extent that we may speak of twin plagues in 2020: one caused by a biological virus, the other by even more contagious viral misconceptions and falsehoods."

256. Shapiro, *The Authoritarian Moment*, 35, "Every offense to particularly 'vulnerable groups'—meaning groups defined as vulnerable by the left in a kaleidoscopically changing hierarchy of victimhood—represents the possibility of profound offense. Those who engage in such offense must be silenced."

Shapiro, *On the Right Side of History*, 15, "The pursuit of individually and communally virtuous goals can only be effectuated when strong social institutions thrive—institutions like churches and synagogues and social clubs and charity organizations--and when government is both strong enough to protect against anarchy and limited enough to check its tendency toward tyranny."

257. Shapiro, *The Authoritarian Moment*, 36, "Subjective perception of offense is quite enough. The culture of microaggression is about magnifying claims of harm in order to gain leverage."

communication censorship. 3) Another occurs as large technological companies privately owned and controlled "borrow" the work of journalists and local media outlets, thus repressing the entrepreneurial spirits of small publishers, newspapers, and independent bookstores. Big Tech gathers into a few hands the means to influence Western democracies negatively and foist totalitarian ends on leadership and people, political philosophies that undermine democracy, limit a free press, and impose thought-control.

As Bottom-Tier residents seek unity and community in echo-chambers, the media monopolies strengthen global empires into entities more powerful than the robber-barons of a previous age. These communication giants control government policies and client interests alike, in the process gathering staggering amounts of data and advertising, wherewith to move covetously in the way of phenomenal self-enrichment, therewith control the political direction of the West.

Control over communication out of Silicon Valley contributes to its prominence, its innovative leaders the envy of other civilizations. However censorship abuse of the media draws Western identity down into the humiliation of arrested development. As the touchstones of Western society fade away, hurried on by Critical Race Theory, many suffer in silence. People who talk to themselves, share private thoughts with pets, or hallucinate example social brokenness passing over the brink into another misdiagnosis of happiness.

Bottom Tier Money

Money lubricates Western civilization, at present incomparably so. At the evident aim of dollar/euro idolatry, ongoing free-market capitalism[258] sets

---

258. Oreskes and Conway, *The Collapse of Western Civilization*, 38, "Market fundamentalism—and its various strands and interpretations known as free market fundamentalism, neoliberalism, laissez-faire economics, and laissez-faire capitalism—was a two-pronged ideological system. The first prong held that societal needs were served most efficiently in a free market economic system. Guided by the 'invisible hand' of the marketplace, individuals would freely respond to each other's needs, establishing a net balance between solutions ("supply") and needs ("demand"). The second prong of the philosophy maintained that free marketers were not merely a good or even the best manner of satisfying material wants: they were the *only* manner of doing so that did not threaten personal freedom."

Ferguson, *Civilization*, 207, "Capitalism inexorably demanded the concentration of capital in ever fewer hands and the reduction of everyone else to wage slavery, which meant being paid only 'that quantum of the means of subsistence which is absolutely

every manner of remuneration—minimum wages, salaries, investments, profits, and honorariums—as high as the traffic will bear,[259] everything adjusted for inflation. In the Bottom-Tier long working hours reflect the ambitions of wealth and the drive to participate in the consumer culture, with disposable income placed at the mercy of the most selfish of gods, Mammon, who adds intrigue to his worship with low interest rates, easy credit, and cheap imports. Mammon-worship inspires determination not to be left behind, impoverished. Enmeshed in the throes of this common religiosity people across a broad spectrum hear the voices of the age; they become what they worship, items, each with a depreciating price tag.

On the debit side of money worship—as debts pile up, overdrafts collect, and credit cards max out—many in monetary crises depend on government bail-out packages or declare bankruptcy to achieve debt reduction. In the dark shadows of financial brokenness live hungry school children, starving seniors, marginalized homeless, and ill-disciplined multitudes unable to budget. Covetousness blinds Westerners to the money god's impotency, a deity that favors the selfish rich. In effect, the monetary fluidity of the West flows away from the poor and selectively enriches upper classes, predictably the Top-Tier powerhouses more so.[260]

Making money draws many into the darkness of the underground activities of counterfeiting. Also here from minor expenses to major financial decisions men and women find the money worth the risk of arrest by border guards and the targeting in crossfires of gang warfare. Actual beneficiaries understandably gather great wealth out of this crime popular in the West and for Westerners. Each violator of this prohibited busyness

---

requisite to keep the labourer in bare existence as a labourer.'"

Hedges, *America*, 177, "Hundreds of millions of people have been severed by modernity from traditions, beliefs, and rituals, as well as communal structures, which kept them rooted. They have been callously cast aside by global capitalism as superfluous. This has engendered an atavistic rage against the technocratic world that condemns them."

Greenspan, *The Age of Turbulence*, 268, "The problem is that the dynamic that defines capitalism, that of unforgiving market competition, clashes with the human desire for stability and certainty."

259. Smith, *A Concise History of New Zealand*, 184, " . . . [New Zealand] continued the Australasian model of state development, whose core business involved managing the economy in an increasingly uncertain and confusing post-war world dominated by the United States."

260. Ferguson, *The Great Degeneration*, 6, "Only by historical methods can we explain why, over the past thirty years, so many countries created forms of debt that, by design, cannot be inflated away, and why, as a result, the next generation will be saddled for life with liabilities incurred by their parents and grandparents."

thinks in a tight circle, I and my needs, without consideration for economic losses to individuals, small businesses, financial institutions, and governments. Since no victims are immediately visible, such as a bloody body, many in the political arena turn a blind eye to this infernal criminality. Counterfeiters along with mules live for themselves, self-righteously, excusing the seriousness of this wrongdoing and refusing to *see* the wounded in the Bottom Tier, a typical Western reaction to fraud-related transgression.

Scamming with its sole aim perpetuates money-games to fleece the unaware, the elderly, and the infirm. Again, scammers, conscienceless in the sociopathic style, have no cares for targets; they perceive only their own wants, tons of wealth for what they perceive as the good life, typically the way of the West.

Intense money hunger on every level bares the Western soul as well as blinds all to the fact that when they thoughtlessly fall over the edge, they have only inert money to hang onto in the unconcealed depths of soul-absorbing redistribution of wealth.[261]

Bottom Tier Pets

Pets—cats, dogs, and other creatures: a multitude of possibilities—give companionship and friendship, the reputations of which highly perched among Western values; for a lot of men and women animals replace children; pets require limited *parental* duties and give unlimited devotion. The company of and care for domestic animals either satisfy procreational urges and/or free owners for carrier building and busy rounds of socializing. However, pet ownership barely hides the fact shared by many that on various levels Westerners find that children prevent access to careers and social liberties; instead of the costly expenses of raising sons and daughters, they companionate in caring for animals.

\/

Poachers and wealthy breeders/sellers of protected species aim at the same goal, more money. Forcing wild animals to behave as pets or as attractions in roadside petting zoos and behind bars makes trafficking in tigers, snakes, and all sorts of profitable wildlife profitably building the crooks' income to levels beyond minimum wages; it enriches breeders/sellers of exotic

---

261. Psalm 119:36, "Incline my heart to your testimonies, and not to selfish gain."

animals with tons of money as well. This shadowy underground industry thrives in the West. In a covert world kingpins, intent on big bucks, breed, show, and sell endangered animal life for medical purposes, aphrodisiacs, or domestication.[262] Westerners true to the spirit of the West find this lucrative business acceptable, abusing creatures meant to live in the wild. The risk of getting caught or hurt takes nothing away from the daring these poachers and traffickers in covert ways expend for money.

Bottom Tier Evolution[263]

In the West at the tip of the evolutionary hypothesis experimenting scientists acting like gods and goddesses by way of invasive or laparoscopic surgeries plan genetic upgrades to the human body as well as the mind, which negates natural selection. Modification technologies and techniques, more eugenics than evolutionary processes, enhance fetuses into designer children, thus preparing another generation for longevity, possibly increasing intelligence and beauty, even possibilities of superhuman abilities. In part, such adaptive surgeries stem from a sense of self-detestation;[264] among the technocratically enabled a festering misanthropy draws many into illusions about human nature physically as well as mentally, even if this produces Frankenstein or mastodon monstrosities. Finding bodies and brains mere pieces of meat for experimentation, surgical and medical adventurists try out investigations with techno-humanism[265] that may, they hope, change

---

262. McKibben, *Falter*, 12, "In fact, *there are half as many wild animals on the planet as there were in 1970*, an awesome and mostly unnoticed silencing."

263. Lindsell, *The New Paganism*, 120, "This theory of how things came into being and how humanoids have developed from lower forms of primate life and ultimately from the first cell has been a part of the enlightenment heritage that has destroyed the *Judeo-Christian Weltanschauung* in the West."

Jones, *Darwin's Ghost*, xviii, "Before Darwin, the great majority of naturalists believed that species were immutable productions, and had been separately created. Today, his theory that they undergo modification and are descendants of previous existing forms is accepted by everyone (or by everyone not determined to disbelieve it)."

264. McKibben, *Falter*, 174–175, "This kind of self-loathing permeates the whole subculture. Robert Ettinger, the first man to start freezing his fellow humans so they could be revived in a century or so, looked forward to a golden posthuman age, one where, among other things, we would be engineered to achieve the 'elimination of elimination.' He found defecation so unpleasant that he wanted 'alternative organs' that would 'occasionally expel small, dry compact residues.'"

265. Harari, *Homo Deus*, 423, "Like all humanist sects, techno-humanism too

people into beautifully arranged beings transiting beyond necessities of plastic surgery, wherefore also experimentation with cryonics.

Bottom Tier Sports

Beyond exercising for personal fitness and socializing in community competitions—baseball, soccer, football, etc.—numerous Westerners long with religious fervors for sportive renown and god-like monetary freedom above and outside racial barriers; these men and women strive for invaluable contractual wealth, thus to attain standing amidst the Top-Tier aristocracy. By participating in professional sports for its financial benefits and basking in its popularity, contestants along with managers struggle for places in winners' circles, the prize the purchase of status in the Top Tier among the movers and shakers of the Western world.

Through the competitors fans pacify deep needs in hero-worship; collaborative devotees of the "idols" find huge satisfaction identifying with and supporting winning teams and champions, willingly paying good money for the successes of the elites.[266]

These greed-centered undertakings, sport participants making money and fans worshipfully laying out money, inspires Westerners in a communal religiosity, hero-worship, that relieves burdens of personal insignificance and life-altering isolation by belonging to a community even if of dubious durability and durable significance. Once over the edge current idols and heroes disappear, forgotten, making room for more totalitarian worshiping.

All involved in *exciting* sports activities, from the professional, to the amateur, to the diverted,[267] find a god-embracing life.

---

sanctifies the human will, seeing it as the nail on which the entire universe hangs. Techno-humanism expects our desires to choose which mental abilities to develop and thereby determine the shape of future minds."

266. Hedges, *America*, 39, "It was what the arena was to ancient Rome, what electronic screens and huge sporting events and concerts are to modernity."

267. Shapiro, *The Authoritarian Moment*, 37, "Culturally apolitical spaces ranging from sports to entertainment have been mobilized on behalf of the Left, weaponized in pursuit of the cultural revolution."

In the West Vertically

Bottom Tier Freedom

Westerners from one end of this civilization to the other yearn for freedom from war, illness, poverty, and racialism,[268] to live in socialistic peace. In this peace they may then exploit money-making sources, after which to relax on the earnings, the goal of Western-oriented work, a work-to-live mentality. In such freedom and with such wealth individuals and families may carry on without a care in the world, the epitome of covetousness. Under these circumstances even wokeists interchange violent dreams for libertarian living. Modernist responsibilities for family, community, nation, and civilization then disintegrate, despite the cosmopolitan identity politics, the strength of woke religiosity.[269]

Human rights activists magnify woke freedom simplistically, to betray Western basics of integrity and dignity; blind to the more abrasive and cruel tyrannies looming over the horizon, they too disappear over the brink from which life no one ever returns.

Bottom Tier Advertising

In this competitive civilization without advertising agencies, businesses on all levels and in every trade relation grind to a halt. Advertising agencies as separate entities represent commercial enterprises and social agencies. To stimulate sales, gain more contracts, and make money for all involved these agencies easily exaggerate the photo-shopped worth of products and services to promote sales, gain more contracts, and make money for all involved.[270] General acceptance of window dressing and welshing on truth in advertising nevertheless strikes at a fundamental of human nature, trust, and thereby reinforces a Western rejection of a noble instinct, integrity, which in whatever next existence over the brink devolves into a vindictively maniacal self-preservation now beyond comprehension.

    268. Streissguth, *Hate Crimes*, 142, racialism: "Claims or views about natural differences in ability or intelligence between members of an ethnic group or nationality."

    269. Fukuyama, *Identity*, 22, "Contemporary identity politics is driven by the quest for equal recognition by groups that have been marginalized by their societies. But that desire for equal recognition can easily slide over into a demand for recognition of the group's superiority."

    270. Harpur, *God Help Us*, 124, 'Much of current marketing research is involved in the sophisticated exploration of where it is that people (always degradingly called 'consumers') feel an itch."

Bottom Tier Persecution

On the right certainly and on the left more, surprisingly many normal Westerners relish conspiracies, endemically so. For one, flimsy conspiracies make more sense out of difficult political currents than reasonable explanations. For up-to-date true believers information about the contents of vaccines, vaccinations and presumed causes of pandemics mean to deceive. For another, irrational reasoning provides pleasure: I am important enough in the universe that something unknown wants (to hurt) me, which excitement alleviates boredom. Partially because of governmental miscommunications, or sometimes due to necessary secrecies, and partially because of political incompetence many otherwise reasonable souls resort to imaginative truthiness and complicated absurdities, exciting means to achieve mental stability within political and social complexities, all too often even in family and neighborhood feuds. Reflection on and participation in such persecution removes tedium from living.

What of actual harassment and discrimination, other than racialized? On the left members of organizations and employees of moneymaking enterprises who refuse to conform to the operative party line find themselves cold-shouldered, in a diversity training program, and/or ejected from membership or employment. Persecutory value judgments also on the right hamper the give-and-take of civilized communication, disallow freedom of thought, and drive unnecessary wedges in a community large or small breaking apart into more baffling fracases of persecution. Hence, factually, birds of a feather flock together, preventing cross-fertilization of ideas and diversity. Right or left, hard lines separate those who belong from those who refuse capitulation to oppressive measures, which autocratic societies impose for mutating the West.

Bottom Tier Culture

Amidst flows of immigrants, streams of migrants, and rifts in left-right diversities, the latter exasperated by Postmodernism, mainstream Westerners consciously or unconsciously *write* a mega-narrative expressive of this in-transition civilization. For emerging into another embodiment of what it means to be the West, the people of this civilization develop a societal and a cultural history of living and dying[271] amidst unforeseen divine scourgings.

---

271. Marsden, *The Twilight of the American Enlightenment*, 8, "Mass culture was

In the West Vertically

Now the West under the revolutionary forces of the masses nears the edge beyond which lurk the troubling revenges of the dying gods and goddesses making place for another pantheon.

America, rather than England and the English Empire, shapes this other narrative, whatever contrarian European, Australasian, or Canadian anti-Americanism. The actual writers and narrators of this chronicling move from Modern illusions into Postmodern woke sensitivities, allegedly seeking the base for a long-lasting civilizational unity, the whole post-racializing, LGBTQ+/LGBTQQIP2AA-accepting, tribalizing, intermarrying, the latter for a "homogenizing humanity."[272] The still current Top-Tier aristocracy prefers this ethno-cultural founding of tomorrow's still faceless people directly distinguishable from pre-Second World War Caucasian dominance and post-Second World War white supremacy;[273] hopefully this congruence of races reestablishes in every future the West's first-among-equals preeminence, the other civilizations agreeing. By mixing into the Western heart racial minorities and hitherto social deviations woke complexities hopefully discover for the West's billions fewer troubling disparities and updated living. Dismantled racialization and forbidden hate crimes[274] lead the West into this another meta-narrative, with basis of union the hard facts of socialism>communism.[275]

---

inevitably degrading, ... unlike folk art, it did not arise from the people but was manufactured and distributed from the top down." "The result was a 'homogenized' culture where everything was mixed together indiscriminately."

272. Ferguson, *Civilization*, 198.
Proser, *Savage Messiah*, 111, quoting a fanatic, "We'll keep bashing the dead White males, and the live ones, and the females too, until the social construct known as the White race is destroyed. Not deconstructed, but destroyed."

273. Mishra, *Bland Fanatics*, 17. "Hysteria about 'white civilisation' gripped America after Europe's self-mutilation in the First World War had encouraged political assertiveness among subjugated peoples from Egypt to China." 48, "This was the prevailing global racial order, built around an exclusionary notion of whiteness and buttressed by imperialism, pseudo-science and the ideology of social Darwinism. In our own time, the steady erosion of the inherited privileges of race has destabilized Western identities and institutions—and it has unveiled racism as an enduringly potent political force, empowering volatile demagogues in the heart of the modern West."

274. Streissguth, *Hate Crimes*, 3, "'Hate crime' as a legal category is a recent invention, but bias-motivated violence has a long history."

275. Shapiro, *The Authoritarian Moment*, 3, "What if, in fact, the most pressing authoritarian threat ... lies precisely with the institutional powers that be: in the well-respected centers of journalism, in the gleaming towers of academia, in the glossy offices of the Hollywood glitterati, in the cubicles of Silicone Valley and the boardrooms of our

Without its global leadership and hard commitment to primacy the West surrenders its battling for international dominance, which decent into meaninglessness leaves future generations mired amidst inconsequential hopes. Everything apart from striving for a better and stronger future, thus to be first among the civilizations, damages the West's Westernism irreparably, its emerging meta-narrative then inconsequential.

Bottom Tier Anti-Americanism

Since the Second World War, fluxes of socialism[276] and communism developed hatred for America's dominance. Rather than thankfulness for helping defeat Nazism and assisting with the subsequent Marshall Plan, socialists/communists regretted the failure of Russia to occupy Europe and create the proletarian state in which governments and party officials provide each according to his/her needs. This anti-Americanism opens doors for totalitarian dictatorships and marks defeats for democratic ideals as wells institutions. Anti-American spirits also affected Pacific Rim countries as New Zealand and Australia that saw American withdrawal from this theatre as a painful rejection of international concerns.[277] In the once defeated socialism>communism (symbolized by the 1991 collapse of the Berlin Wall) a new generation finds dictatorial stability more appealing than friction-full and obsolescing democracy.

---

corporate behemoths?"

276. Packer and Howard, *Christianity*, 21, "Politically, most Western humanists embrace some kind of egalitarian socialism. Where Marxism subordinates the individual to community interests and existentialism dissects and mocks him as a passionate absurdity, Anglo-American humanism treats personal welfare as the ultimate value and leaves each individual as free as possible to define welfare for himself in egotistic terms—comfort, convenience, aesthetic pleasure, affluence, self-improvement, sexual satisfaction according to taste, and so on."

Lindsell, *The New Paganism*, 130, "All forms of socialism, whether utopian or Marxist, have in mind the desire to establish an egalitarian society in which economic and political distinction are broken down so that all are equal."

277. Smith, *A Concise History of New Zealand*, 184–185, " . . . the nation faced the 'Anzac dilemma', of having to juggle the expectations of not one but two great power protectors as a result of World War II. To confound the dilemma, the less preferred protector, the United States, was now the dominant Pacific power, replacing Britain, which was in withdrawal and decline."` "The United States, however, was less intimate and familiar, and played by different rules, as yet unknown. 'Do as we say' appeared to be the directive."

In the West VERTICALLY

ASSIMILATIVE THOUGHTS

Slowly, imperceptibly the West moves into soft totalitarianism to establish beyond even woke characterization another identity.[278] What communism failed at delivering in Russia and throughout Eastern Europe, communists now toying with socialism mean to morph the West into a work of totalitarian monstrosity, first with pleasing propaganda in a tension-weary Occident. In a civilization shredding with economic inequalities, poisoned by partisan gridlock, and weary of political violence, the narcissism of self-destruction in tyranny calls from the bottom of the Western heart. Warnings of damnation in the second and last Judgment fall on deaf ears.

\/

As you see yourselves in these fMRI files walking over the edge into dystopian worlds, self-examination in the light of the Word ought to be a foremost preoccupation, like breathing, or face total damnation. Again, within self-examination shines the future of Jesus' Second Advent. Put it this way: if the West rather than the Scriptures shapes and fills your hearts the hour for radical sanctification is now. The further you are estranged from the Kingdom and the deeper you are immersed in Westernism, the more desperate now the return home, following the prodigal son, Luke 15:11–32.

At odds with secularization, being different, excites unease; it is easier to assimilate by way of the migratory order than to explain Christianity's way, despite 1 Peter 3:15; the discomfort of clarifying the work of the Kingdom and membership in the Church persuades moving within egalitarian socialism and the distribution of allegiances, one in the Christ and the other to the world. In this hypocrisy for now difficult questions are warded off in favor of naturally gliding down into deep darkness. Easing into enculturation is much less painful, quietly spurning the will of the Lord Jesus by approving Westernism congregationally and individually. Since accommodation is easier and immediately more gratifying than Christian gratitude for the Atonement, the way away from the Faith gains the love of hearts, minds, and souls growing cold.

As accurate fMRI files identify you on the migratory order and uncover your temptations and intrigues of imagination, these bare the trap(s)

---

278. Shapiro, *On the Right Side of History*, xxv, "Our way of life is never more than one generation away from the precipice."

Self-Examination

you are in or demonstrate your pride in Westernism, then one other fact stands out: the hour of self-examination quickly passes by.

FINALLY

THE QUIVERING FUTURE OPENING for the West comes with hopes and dreams for preeminence among the earth's civilizations and cultures; these hopes and dreams interact daily with rambunctious ferments of revolt for Postmodern relativities and wokeist fractures. However, amidst anticipation and imagining Westerners find themselves a spurned people, subject to plundering.

As the West for now devolves into one among others, those from other cultures and civilizations, including wokeism, want its material wealth to gain the stability and the equality that Western moneys buy, but in a de-racialized world. As the West's centuries-old primacy falls away, anti-Occidentals prey on its immeasurable wealth. For who can estimate the worth of trillions upon trillions of dollars and euros? The rivals, however, want it all. Look up the nearest four-lane and see now into tomorrow predations.

International powers and internal operatives hunger and thirst for the external advantages the West flaunts by way of communication media; they seek participation only in its wealth and the life money buys, which the aristocracy and Bottom-Tier upper-classes parade[1] across digital screens. East Asians, Africans, South Americans, aboriginals, and woke operatives

---

1. Ferguson, *Civilization*, 7, "Only a few societies continue to resist the encroachment of Western patterns of marketing and consumption, as well as the Western lifestyle itself. More and more human beings eat a Western diet, wear Western clothing and live in Western housing." 197–198, "What is it about our clothes that other people seem unable to resist? Is dressing like us about wanting to *be* like us? Clearly, this is about more than just clothes. It is about embracing an entire popular culture that extends through music and movies, to say nothing of soft drinks and fast food. That popular culture carries with it a subtle message. It is about freedom—the right to dress or drink or eat as you please (even if that turns out to be like everybody else). It is about democracy—because only those consumer products that people really like get made."

Harpur, *God Help Us*, 17, "The gap between rich and poor, even in the so-called First World, including the richest country of all, the United States—is still widening apace."

despise the West's personality; they vilify the West for its colonizing and empire-building proclivities,[2] for military and economic weights thrown about. From across the globe people at best despise Westerners while confiscating this civilization's material goods and superior technologies from under its still towering figure of domination. Critical loss of primacy globally reshapes the West's intercontinental stature.[3] From outside orbits, primarily Russian, Chinese, and Muslim, and inside socialist powers rise up against each other and the West to shift the globe as a whole into unknown priorities. As these other forces, lusting for power, spread abroad they compel the West into the cage of a descending elevator.

V

Within Western boundaries self-same hatreds as found abroad boil up out of this civilization's soul. 1) Bureaucrats with socialist micro-managing skills repress Western initiatives and excite woke spirits, sucking the life blood out of the West; following the worn-out tracks of communism they eye a utopia on the horizon peopled by zombies. Bureaucratic managers of Western ambitions resemble box-store managers utterly devoid of interest in the wellsprings of community.[4] 2) By over-organizing bureaucracies they trap fellow citizens in steely cobwebs and imprisoning chains to restrict Westerners' entrepreneurial genius: impersonal rules, casuistic authorities, and feckless powers move these over-paid administrators to clamp down on Western freedoms. 3) With the density and intensity of Rev. Jeremiah Wright (1941–?),[5] *Black Lives Matter,* and *Antifa* hordes, racial minorities damn first America and in the process the entire West. To erase

---

2. Hedges, *America*, 39, "Its complexity mandates a permanent cast of bureaucrats and military leaders who strip the citizenry of power."

3. Huntington, *The Clash of Civilizations*, 29, "The West is and will remain for years to come the most powerful civilization. Yet its power relative to that of other civilizations is declining."

4. Ferguson, *Civilization*, 151, "Man, Rousseau argued, is a 'noble savage' who is reluctant to submit to authority. The only legitimate authority to which he can submit is the sovereignty of 'the People' and the "General Will'. According to Rousseau, that General Will must be supreme."

Fukuyama, *Identity*, 30, " . . . Rousseau argued that that the first human being—man in the state of nature—was *not* sinful. The characteristics we associate with sin and evil—jealousy, greed, violence, hatred, and the like—did not characterize the earliest humans."

5. Shapiro, *The Authoritarian Moment*, 60, "It was no surprise that [Barack Obama] gravitated to Jeremiah Wright, attending his church for twenty years, listening to him spew bile from the pulpit about the evils of the United States."

racial inequalities, these destructive forces build a cultural crisis with which to salvage minorities' resilience, therewith to change forever more than the face of the West, also its global position among civilizations. Throughout the West now anti-Western spirits—terribly Postmodernist— undermine this Renaissance>Enlightenment>Modernist civilization.

\/

As the West descends into distress of soul—lost in self-righteousness and losing the will to live—crises (as the 2019–2022 coronavirus pandemic) uncover confusion in authority. In this Anthropocene age, with too many authorities calling for this solution and advising that resolution, a hunger arises for a dictatorial voice to set matters right. As this civilizational thrust concentrates in externalities, crises move in and about destructively, inward, to haunt the present with past mistakes. Relief from this guilt the *compelling advantages* offer, surrendering leadership to technocrats, and stuffing the future with conspiracies.[6] In other words, as long as Westerners concentrate on replicating the wealth of aristocrats in personal bank accounts with arch-villainous money hungers, they immobilize democratic freedoms. While Western paganization deepens, recorded troubling of soul in the West's in-process meta-narrative will distress generations yet unborn.[7]

Soon comes the Second Advent in which the glorious Christ, the Judge of heaven and earth, demonstrates publicly the end of all Westerners' results at self-esteem and its misery, the whole born out of self-righteousness. At the collective reckoning Jesus hands down the salvation and the damnation created in the first and great Judgment. Therefore, James 5:9, let it be known that the Judge stands at the door.

---

6. Shapiro, *On the Right Side of History*, xxvi, "Our civilization is riddled with internal contradictions, communities bereft of values, and individuals bereft of meaning."

7. Ferguson, *Doom*, 1, "Never in our lifetime, it seems, has there been greater uncertainty about the future—and greater ignorance of the past."

Bibliography

Abrahamian, Ervand, *A History of Modern Iran*, New York: Cambridge University Press, 2008.
Applebaum, Anne, *Twilight of Democracy: The Seductive Lure of Authoritarianism*, Toronto: Penguin/Random House, 2020.
Arnold, Catharine, *Pandemic 1918: Eyewitness Accounts From the Greatest Medical Holocaust In Modern Times*, New York: St. Martin's, 2018.
Bonhoeffer, Dietrich, tr. Eberhard Bethge. *Ethics*, New York: Macmillan, 1949/1970.
Boyd, Neil, *Canadian Law: An Introduction*, 5th ed., Toronto: Nelson, 2011.
Buchanan, Pat, *The Death of the West: How Dying Populations and Immigrant Invasions Imperil Our Country*, New York: St Martin's Griffin, 2001.
Campbell, Joseph, *The Masks of God: Primitive Mythology*, New York: Penguin, 1959/78.
Carson, Rachel, *Silent Spring*, Greenwich, Conn: Fawcett, 1962.
Dreher, Rod, *Live Not by Lies: A Manual for Christian Dissidents*, Toronto: Sentinel/Penguin, 2020.
Du Bois, W.E.B., *The Souls of Black Folk*, New York: Bantam, 1903/1989.
Ferguson, Niall, *Civilization: The West and the Rest*, New York: Penguin, 2011.
———. *Doom: The Politics of Catastrophe*, New York: Penguin, 2021.
———. *The Great Degeneration: How Institutions Decay and Economies Die*, New York: Penguin, 2012.
Fukuyama, Francis, *Identity: the Demand for Dignity and the Politics of Resentment*, New York: Farrar, Straus and Giroux, 2018.
Gillam, Carey, *Whitewash: The Story of a Weed Killer, Cancer, and the Corruption of Science*, Washington: Island Press, 2017.
Greenspan, Alan, *The Age of Turbulence: Adventures In a New World*, New York: Penguin, 2007.
Harari, Yuval Noah, *Homo Deus: A Brief History of Tomorrow*, Toronto: Signal, 2015.
Harpur, Tom, *God Help Us*, Toronto: McClelland & Stewart, 1992.
Hazard, Paul, *The European Mind: 1680-1715*, New York: World Publishing, 1963/1968.
Hedges, Chris, *America, The Farewell Tour*, Toronto: Knopf Canada, 2018.
Huntington, Samuel P., *The Clash of World Civilizations and the Remaking of the World Order*, New York: Simon & Schuster, 1996.
Jones, Steve, *Darwin's Ghost: The Origin of Species Updated*, Toronto: Anchor Canada, 1999.
Lindsell, Harold, *The New Paganism: Understanding American Culture & The Role of the Church*, San Francisco: Harper & Row, 1987.

Bibliography

Manthorpe, Jonathan, *Claws of the Panda: Beijing's Campaign of Influence and Intimidation in Canada*, Toronto: Cormorant, 2019.

Marsden, George M., *The Twilight of the American Enlightenment: The 1950s and the Crisis of Liberal Belief*, New York: Basic Books, 2014.

McKibben, Bill, *Falter: Has the Human Game Begun to Play Itself Out?*, New York: Henry Hold and Company, 2019.

Mishra, Pankaj, *Bland Fanatics: Liberals, Race, and Empire*, New York: Farrar, Straus and Giroux, 2020.

Morgan, Kenneth, *Australia: A Very Short Introduction*, Oxford: Oxford University Press, 2012.

Oreskes, Naomi and Erick M. Conway, *The Collapse of Western Civilization: A View From the Future*, New York: Columbia University Press, 2014.

Packer, J.I. and Thomas Howard, *Christianity: the True Humanism*, Waco: Word, 1985.

Packer, J.I., *A Quest for Godliness: The Puritan Vision of the Christian Life*, Wheaton: Crossway, 1990.

Proser, Jim, *Savage Messiah: How Dr. Jordan Peterson Is Saving Western Civilization*, New York: St. Martin's, 2019.

Rand, Ayn, ed. *The Virtue of Selfishness: A New Concept of Egoism*, Toronto: Signet, 1964/1969.

Rogan, Eugene, *The Arabs: A History*, New York: Basic Books, 2009.

Saul, John Ralston, *The Unconscious Civilization* (The 1995 Massey Lectures), Toronto: Anansi, 1995.

Schell, Jonathan, *The Fate of the Earth*, New York: Avon, 1982.

Shapiro, Ben, *Primetime Propaganda: The True Hollywood Story of How the Left Took Over Your TV*, New York: Broadside/HarperCollins, 2011.

———. *The Right Side of History: How Reason and Moral Purpose Made the West Great*, New York: Broadside/HarperCollins, 2019.

———. *The Authoritarian Moment: How the Left Weaponized America's Institutions Against Dissent*, New York: Broadside/HarperCollins, 2021.

Smith, James K.A., *Who's Afraid of Postmodernism: Taking Derrida, Lyotard, and Foucault to Church*, Grand Rapids: Baker Academic, 2006.

Smith, Philippa Mein, *A Concise History of New Zealand*, Cambridge: Cambridge University Press, 2012.

Spinney, Laura, *Pale Rider: The Spanish Flue of 1918 and How It Changed the World*, New York: Public Affairs, 2017.

Stein, Mark, *Lights Out: Islam, free speech and the twilight of the west*, Woodsville, New Hampshire: Stockade Books, 2009.

Streissguth, Tom, *Hate Crimes: Library In a Book*, New York: Facts On File, 2003/2009.

Tenold, Vegas, *Everything You Love Will Burn: Inside the Rebirth of White Nationalism in America*, New York: Nation Books, 2018.

Thatcher, Margaret, *The Downing Street Years*, New York: HarperCollins, 1993.

Thunberg, Greta, *No One Is Too Small To Make a Difference*, New York: Penguin, 2018-2019.

Toynbee, Arnold J., *Civilization On Trial*, New York: Oxford University Press, 1948.

Winchester, Simon, *Pacific: Silicon Chips and Surfboards, Coral Reefs and Atom Bombs, Fading Empires, and the Coming Collision of the World's Superpowers*, New York: Harper, 2015.

www.ingramcontent.com/pod-product-compliance
Lightning Source LLC
Chambersburg PA
CBHW070915160426
43193CB00011B/1465